BACK TO THE 50'S

IMPACT ON THE ILLINOIS VALLEY

By
R. G. Bluemer

Published by Grand Village Press
134 Cleveland Circle
Granville, IL 61326
© 2010
Printing
MCS Advertising - Peru, IL
ISBN 978-0-615-35827-7

The material found in this work was primarily derived from information found in the following newspapers: LaSalle News-Tribune, Ottawa Republican Times, Bureau County Republican, Wenona Index, Dixon Telegraph, and Putnam County Record. Additional information was obtained from personal interviews with individuals who experienced the actual events and relatives of those individuals.

1950
A RETURN TO PEACE

The end of World War II brought hope for a new era of peace and prosperity in the turbulent history of the world. The troops were returning to America back to joyful family reunions. After being discharged, many veterans anticipated a return to their civilian jobs or took advantage of the G. I. Bill of Rights and enrolled in a college or technical school to further their education. Others looked forward to marriage and raising a family in one of the new bungalows in the sprawling suburbs.

However, those expectations were tempered even in the closing days of the war by the ominous growth of world communism emanating from Stalin's Soviet Union and Mao Tse Tung's Red China. The secrets of the atomic bomb were soon compromised, and the use of nuclear weapons as well as conventional armaments increased world tensions. Those threats in the last half of the 1940's became even more apparent with the Soviet's challenge to the Allied occupation of Germany with the Berlin Blockade. Although that particular threat was eliminated with the success of the year-long Berlin Airlift, it became obvious that the peace, so long sought for by Americans, might be only a dream.

For those living in the Illinois Valley, many of these new threats were viewed only as distant international news and of little concern in their everyday lives. The fighting in Europe and the Pacific had been over for five years. Concerns had shifted from the wartime draft and inconvenience of ration stamps for food, clothing, and gasoline to focusing on the purchase of a new car, a first house and the multitude of newly designed appliances, especially black and white televisions.

Weekend entertainment included a night at the movies, which featured American westerns, comedies, and a continued flow of wartime-inspired motion pictures. Hundreds of bars and restaurants that lined the main streets of towns large and small offered refreshments and entertainment ranging from big band dances to taking a chance on slot machines, punch boards, and other types of gambling.

The newest changes in automotive designs and innovations were eagerly awaited every year during the decade. This ad from the Ottawa Republican Times in January 1950 illustrates one of the 19 models of new Chryslers available at the Pool and Pool dealership in Ottawa.

LaSalle in particular became a mecca for out-of-towners, who traveled from Chicago aboard the Rock Island and

booked rooms at the Kaskaskia Hotel for a weekend of musical entertainment, good food, and gambling at one of the city's well-known casinos, such as the Silver Congo and Kelly-Cawley's. There were plenty of clubs, bars, and restaurants in the Illinois Valley, such as the Paddock in Streator, the Rose Bowl in LaSalle, and South Bluff country club across the river from Peru, where both local residents and tourists spent their time. These businesses were well-established before the 1950's, but it was in that decade they prospered and raised such concerns among some community leaders that war was unofficially declared on their operations. The battle did not begin with a specific event or historic date, but it was a war nonetheless with the goal of stamping out what some determined to be not only illegal but also an offense to their sensibilities of propriety.

There were other concerns during the decade. The polio epidemic that began in the late 40's – hitting epidemic proportions in 1949 – continued into the next decade. The March of Dimes would be an annual January fundraiser for years to come. Dime-holders were distributed to children and adults encouraging contributions to stamp out the dreaded disease. There were many citywide celebrations and other forms of entertainment to distract individuals from the war in Korea, nuclear testing, and even imagined threats from aliens in flying saucers. However, for the most part, normalcy and a peaceful lifestyle had returned to the Illinois Valley.

In early January 1950, the Chicago Tribune began an advertising campaign in the Illinois Valley newspapers to encourage readers to follow the adventures of Hopalong Cassidy, a new feature beginning on Jan. 4, 1950 in the Tribune's daily comic section. The appeal to purchase a copy of the Windy City newspaper had a local impact in several respects. Streator was the birthplace of the creator of the western hero. Clarence Mulford (right) was born in 1883 and wrote 28 books detailing the exploits of Hopalong Cassidy. The unusual name for Mulford's fictitious, hard-drinking cowboy came from a gunshot wound  in his left leg that left him with a limp. Mulford began his series of novels with the publication of "Bar 20" in 1907. His last novel, "Hopalong Cassidy Serves a Writ," was published in 1941.

Mulford's books served as the basis for the 66 movies produced in the 1930's through the 1950's. The first film, "Hop-Along Cassidy," was released in 1935. Ironically, Mulford refused to meet with William Boyd, the actor who was the star of the movies. The film director insisted on recasting Boyd as an upright man of honor instead of the rough and tumble cowboy created by Mulford.

The imagination of youngsters was rejuvenated by a Hopalong Cassidy radio series that began in 1948 and lasted until 1951. The western hero was also seen on half-hour television episodes in the 1950's. Although dressed completely in black, viewers quickly recognized William Boyd as the hero. His attire stood out in comparison to contemporary cowboy heroes, who traditionally wore white hats.

Capitalizing on the popularity of the legendary cowboy, a variety of marketing endeavors brought profits even to local businesses. For example, the Wilcox Paint and Linoleum store at 225 W. Madison in Ottawa advertised Hopalong Cassidy wallpaper to encourage mothers to redecorate the children's rooms for as little as $8.50.

William Boyd endorsed 2,400 different products. This artwork used for the Wilcox store ad appeared in the April 21, 1950 edition of the Ottawa Republican Times. At Christmas 1950, Hopalong Cassidy radios were available at the Hentrick Music House in Ottawa for $17.95. In 2009, that same model radio was offered on eBay for $800! The Streator Historical Society has an assortment of Hopalong Cassidy collectibles including books, records, and even a 16 mm movie.

Mulford died in 1956 but remained a historic figure in Streator for his creation of the Western hero. The Hopalong Cassidy River Trail along the Vermilion River in Streator takes hikers past Mulford's house.

Streator Historical Society photo.

Another author of a notable western figure, Zorro, was Johnston McCulley, who was born in Ottawa on Feb. 2, 1883. His family moved, and he was raised in Chillicothe, IL. McCulley's first account of Zorro, "The Curse of Capistrano," appeared in a pulp fiction weekly magazine in 1919. McCulley died on Nov. 23, 1958.

The enthusiasm for Westerns grew in Ottawa, when the Republican Times ran an article about a future movie titled "Rock Island Trail." The reason for the interest was that the producers used a replica of Ottawa's Rock Island depot as one of the sets, where senatorial candidate Abe Lincoln was portrayed leaving the train in Ottawa for one of his historic debates with Senator Stephen Douglas. During the months before the premiere showing in Ottawa, the local businesses got behind an effort to make the opening a memorable event for the entire community.

THE COAL WAR

The casual lifestyle in the Illinois Valley was gradually affected by a national coal miners' strike, which began in early January in the eastern coalfields. John L. Lewis, president of the United Mine Workers (UMW), advised the miners to go back to work on Jan. 11, but they refused. Even a threat by President Truman to use the provisions of the Taft-Hartley Act and the issuance of a 10-day back to work order by a federal judge had no effect.

The main issue in the Truman-Lewis "coal war," pitting the president against the UMW union, was money. The miners pay was $14.05 per day with a 20-cent welfare tonnage royalty. The UMW wanted a 95-cent per day raise and an additional 35-cents welfare tonnage royalty. That would raise salaries to about $15 per day. The union leadership also wanted a guaranteed 200-day work year to stabilize employment. However, Lewis explained that those demands were the top limits and subject to negotiation.

The strike in the Eastern coalfields raised concerns among Illinois Valley leaders almost immediately. Just before the Christmas holidays, the Marseilles school district received a carload of stoker coal. However, in early January, School Superintendent Clyde Crawshaw cautioned that amount would only last for a month, assuming normal winter weather conditions occurred. National Biscuit Carton Co. in Marseilles consumed about 150 tons of coal every day and only had a two-week supply on hand. When that was gone, layoffs would follow. The Certain-Teed plant had a three-week supply of screenings shipped to Marseilles from Fiatt, IL. The coal mine was located southwest of Peoria in Fulton County.

The National Biscuit Carton plant in Marseilles was ready to close in February 1950 because of the coal shortages. Photo by author.

Newspaper stories began to panic homeowners, who were placing orders with local coal companies with increasing frequency hoping to have enough coal to keep their families from freezing.

By mid-January, the ICC announced the possible elimination of two of the four daily passenger trains on the Streator-Aurora branch because of the coal strike. The only Burlington passenger trains would be the evening southbound and the morning northbound trains.

Ottawa also would have mail service with the No. 6 eastbound Rock Island train at 3:55 a.m. and the No. 9 westbound train at 3 a.m. There were still westbound streamliners passing through Ottawa: the No. 501 at 11:55 a.m. and the No. 503 at 8:19 p.m. The eastbound Rock Island Rockets would stop at Ottawa three times a day.

Although the strike was concentrated in Pennsylvania and West Virginia coalfields, not all miners belonged to the UMW. A rival organization, the Progressive Mine Workers Union, did not participate in the walkout. These union miners produced about one-fifth of Illinois coal supply.

More local closures were announced on Jan. 27. Although the Utica school board was making every effort to locate coal supplies, they were forced to close the village school. However, if coal could be purchased over the weekend, the board decided to open the building on Monday.

The situation was not as desperate for other buildings. The Irwin School east of Utica on Rt. 6 and the French School had sufficient coal on hand. However, the Lone Tree School on Rt. 6 burned oil instead of coal so there was no danger of canceling classes.

Local business owners were more concerned about their coal stockpiles. Only one coal gondola had carried a supply to the Utica Elevator since Dec. 1. According to owner Adolph Jesse, the Illinois Valley Grain Elevator was in a similar situation,

Utica township supervisor Dee Bennett said that the Osage Mine was cooperating as much as possible, but mud and water were hindering operations. In spite of those problems, there was some coal for families on relief. The maximum allotment was 50-75 pounds. Other coal was being supplied by a small mine in Lowell.

The dwindling supply of coal for school and other institutions began to have a major impact by February. Several of the state colleges announced closings. These included Northern Illinois State Teachers College, Eastern Illinois State College, Illinois Normal College, and Western Illinois State College.

Soon, the situation grew more serious in the Illinois Valley. On Feb. 9, O. H. Lewis, the warden at the state reformatory at Sheridan, reported they only had 10-12 days of coal remaining. He was doubtful of getting even a single carload. He told a Times reporter the trains were "snatching it enroute to keep their trains running." They were trying to conserve coal at the reformatory and the large employees' dormitory located two miles to the south of the reformatory.

LaSalle county institutions were also experiencing severe difficulties. Occasional carloads of coal made it possible to operate the LaSalle County Home, located west of Ottawa, but only on a day-by-day basis. They typically used 1,200 tons per year and kept the boilers fired every day.

The LaSalle County Home survived the shortage. Photo by author.

Miss Esther Roach, superintendent of the LaSalle detention home, said that their situation was not as serious. They still had a two-week supply on hand. The LaSalle county courthouse and jail were in dire straits. According to Sheriff Edward Ryan, they were depending on coal deliveries from a Streator company, and operations continued on a day-to-day basis. Miss B. Chapman, superintendent of the county tuberculosis sanitarium, also depended on the same Streator supplier to keep her institution operating.

Local industries were also in trouble. Henry Thornton of Ottawa Silica announced it would be closing operations on Feb. 17 if more coal was unavailable for the power plant. Company reserves were down to an eight-day supply. Barge deliveries of coal at this point were "practically nothing at all" according to the Republican Times.

Two other companies, Libby-Owens-Ford Glass in west Ottawa and the Bakelite Company on Rt. 6, had enough coal for another 18-20 days. Neither R.R. Nickerson, manager of L-O-F, nor A. B. Dickinson, speaking on behalf of the Bakelite Company, would give a specific closing date as did Ottawa Silica. The company representatives said if they were forced to close, the date would be around the same time as the silica operation. Together, L-O-F and Bakelite employed 1,860 workers.

Alpha Cement in LaSalle laid off workers due to a lack of coal for the kilns in 1950. Photo by author.

With serious unemployment conditions facing Ottawa, the news of the three major employers was keenly watched. On Thursday, Feb. 16, Thornton told the Times enough coal had been received to keep operations going for another week and a half. Dickinson reported that the coal supply would likely last only until Mar. 1. L-O-F reported an 18-day supply.

The local cement companies, which used large quantities of coal, were also in trouble. On Feb. 16, Alpha Portland Cement in LaSalle announced that 175 workers would be laid off since the plant was shutting down operations at 7 a.m. on Sat. Feb. 18. It was the first shutdown in about seven years according to the Republican Times. Marquette Cement in Oglesby was only running at half its capacity.

Bad news was also reported from Wedron, IL. Albert Dietman, office manager of Wedron Silica, said their supply was reaching the point where they would have to close unless more coal became available within ten days.

With only a 10-day supply of coal, Wedron Silica came close to suspending operations in February 1950. Photo by author.

The sister superior of St. Joseph's Health resort said they had a two-three week supply of coal. She considered the situation "fortunate" because of the bad road conditions caused by the snow and ice storm that blanketed the area the previous Sunday.

The coal war was spreading. The Wallace Grain and Supply Co. on Rt. 6 had sent empty gondolas down to Athens, IL, but the plant manager, Paul Doherty, thought they would come back empty. About 3,000 miners from the Progressive Mine Workers in southern Illinois had gone on strike.

The Conco-Meier Brick operation in Lowell was one of the few companies that fared better than most. In the fall of 1949, they had ordered a large supply of coal for their kilns in anticipation of the coal strike. According to Otto Elligen, the plant manager, they had enough coal to last until Mar. 16.

The employment concerns were only one of several problems facing the Illinois Valley. Keeping the children in schools without heat was another worry. The Rutland school board was forced to close its grade school for an indefinite period. Students at Ottawa Township H.S. went on a shortened schedule. According to Supt. MacRae Shannon, classes would last 40 minutes, and the school day would begin at 9:45 a.m. and end at 2:44 p.m. One concern was the possibility of eliminating all lunch periods if all of the students could not be fed in the time available. Jefferson School was down to a single day's supply of coal.

Priority coal deliveries were being instituted for certain institutions. The director of Ryburn-King Hospital in Ottawa reported they were down to only two-three days of coal. Heat for the nuns' quarters at Marquette H.S. was another priority.

The terrible winter weather in the Illinois Valley compounded the coal emergency. A third day of sleet and snow on Wednesday, Feb. 15 created major difficulties for power and light companies. In Bureau County, ice covered tree limbs crashed down on power lines cutting service. The LaMoille-Tiskilwa basketball game was cancelled due to the lack of power, and Mineral H.S. closed the following Monday for the same reason.

The French Coal Co. near Kangley agreed to deliver coal to the Highland sanitarium and the detention home, but local schools were not deemed critical users.

On Friday, Feb. 17, Father David Duncan, rector at St. Bede College and Academy, suspended classes, sending home 350 students. This included all the student boarders. For those students from China, Cuba, and Mexico, arrangements were made so they could stay with friends in America until the emergency ended. There was still concern for the 50 priests and 13 nuns, who resided at the monastery. "It's going to be a rather chilly Friday afternoon," Duncan said to a News Tribune reporter. A concert planned for the following Sunday was also cancelled. However, the home basketball game between St. Bede and Rock Island Alleman for Feb 19 and the away game at Ottawa Township on Feb. 21 were not cancelled.

St. Bede Academy was closed in February 1950 due to the national coal strike.

Locally, the situation was reaching a critical state. On Feb. 21, Ottawa School Supt. Warren Shepherd announced the indefinite closing of all grade schools effective at the conclusion of classes on Feb. 22. "Our supply (of coal) is dangerously low, and our source of supply is down to zero. The coal we have on hand is being used to protect buildings. The schools will be closed tomorrow night and will remain closed until further notice," he told a Republican Times reporter.

As for the local high schools, Marquette and Ottawa Township, and the parochial grade schools, St. Columba, St. Pat's, and St. Francis, were expected to operate with shortened days to conserve coal. Half-day schedules at the Ottawa high schools were sufficient to count as full days for the requirements of the states so that there would be no need to extend the school year into the summer of 1951.

On Feb. 22, Hall H.S. followed St. Bede's example and suspended classes. Principal Cecil Sharpe made the announcement as directed by the school board since the coal supply had dropped to less than ten tons. The remainder was necessary to generate sufficient heat to prevent damage to the building. In addition, the adult agriculture classes were suspended until further notice.

Classes were still being conducted in DePue, but Superintendent Ray Stutz cautioned that there was only enough coal for about ten days. Without more deliveries, the school would have to close in another week.

At Immaculate Conception School in Spring Valley, Father Ralph E. Gates said that he was closing the school effective Feb. 23. Parishioners would find the church itself was only being heated to 50 degrees. The coal supplies at the Lincoln and Grant Schools in Spring Valley were down to five and eight days respectively. That would not be enough to keep classes in session for an entire week since some coal would still be needed to maintain minimal heat for the buildings.

There was little hope for additional supplies in Spring Valley. The manger of the Hunter, Doherty, and Co, lumberyard described the situation as "the worst ever" to a Spring Valley Gazette reporter. Only one coal car arrived at the yard on Wednesday. That small amount was being rationed for emergency needs only. None was delivered to individuals who had any coal left in their coal bin. Truck drivers were instructed to look in a person's coal bin before unloading. For those who had nothing, they could only hope for a maximum 500-pound delivery from the Spring Valley coal dealer.

The Princeton city council authorized Mayor K. M. Nelson to issue orders to conserve coal. On Feb. 20, the mayor responded with a resolution asking for the voluntary conservation of coal. The city power plant only had sufficient coal for 14 days. City lighting was immediately reduced by 50 percent. All unnecessary display and advertising lighting was to be eliminated as well.

The Princeton library board also took action. G. P. Seibel, president of the board, announced that the Matson Public Library would close until the coal emergency ended.

LaSalle-Peru H.S. and L-F-O Junior College were also forced to shorten schedules effective Wednesday, Feb. 29. The school board decided it was in the best interests of the community to adjust the school day from noon to 4 p.m. Instead of classes meeting for 50 minutes, they would be in session only for 25 minutes, The typical class spent half the time in recitation and the remaining time in supervised study. The changes were designed to simply eliminate the supervised study portion of the class. The board assumed that students would use their mornings to study at home.

The LaSalle grade schools, which were currently operating on a half-day schedule, were not about to be totally suspended as rumors suggested. According to superintendent E.G. Miller, there was adequate coal on hand to continue an abbreviated schedule "indefinitely."

By instituting the new measures, large quantities of coal would be saved and made available for home consumption. Tom Flannery, the building superintendent, told the board that there was plenty of coal in the bins, enough for at least the next two weeks. Cutting the school day to four hours and ceasing all coal stoking to the boilers at 3:30 p.m. would save even more coal.

Evening classes at the L-P-O junior college would not be affected by the cessation of stoking in the afternoon; the rooms would remain warm. The board also decided not to rent the Matthiessen Memorial auditorium for evening events until the crisis abated. By shortening the school day, the board felt the school could avoid a total closure if the strike was prolonged.

More industries were affected the following week after the ICC ordered Illinois power plants to decrease electrical output by 25 percent. Spring Valley merchants and shop owners did their part by turning off all window and store lighting. City officials decided to restrict street lighting by extinguishing all but one fixture on each street corner. The Spring Valley Gazette noted it was like wartime conditions.

Industries responded by cutting production. Five local companies, employing over 3,000 workers, quickly adjusted their production schedules. These included two Streator companies, G & D, manufacturers of farm implements, and Owens-Illinois Glass. In Ottawa, Bakelite Corp., Peltiers Glass, and J.E. Porter Corp. changed their routines. Duncan Peltier said his company would begin a four-day week to meet the ICC requirement. At the J.E. Porter Corp., management decided to close the plant on Saturday and Sunday. Their 110 employees were told not to report for the usual half-day operation on Saturday. Bakelite had enough coal to operate until Mar. 10. However, the electrical restrictions mandated changing the daily work schedule to four six-hour shifts. According to R. F. Picard, this would allow for an equitable distribution of the working time.

Three other major industries, Standard Silica, Wedron Silica, and Chicago Retort and Fire Brick Co., complied without resorting to shortened schedules. Chicago Retort was in a rather unique situation since it had a backup oil-fired electric plant. The company president, Charles S. Reed Jr., also noted there was a layer of low-grade coal overlying the clay beds they mined. Although he didn't want to use that coal, he said they would do just that because of the current emergency. This move would make it possible, according to Reed, to share some of the 100 tons of coal it normally ordered from southern Illinois mines with Ottawa coal dealers.

In spite of school and industry closings, the miners refused to go back to work. Their slogan was "No contract, no work." When federal judge Richard Keech issued a no-strike order, John L. Lewis advised the miners to go back to the mines. In spite of their leader's admonition, they still refused.

The national situation grew worse by the day. In Pittsburgh, the state police escorted truckers hauling coal into the city. Picketers had thrown rocks at coal haulers smashing several truck windows.

Conditions were never that dangerous in the Illinois Valley. Managers at the Scoog and Stuart independent mine located about a mile west of Ottawa on Moriarty Hill agreed to furnish Ottawa with coal on Feb. 26. The mine, which had been leased from the Osage Coal Co., had closed for 59 days in the fall of 1949 due to a strike, but was back in operation using independent miners.

The company was a small strip mine employing only 12 men from Ottawa and Utica. On a good day, the mine's stripping machine could operate 24 hours a day digging out the 21-inch seam, which was located 35-40 feet below the surface. However, even with continuous mining, the entire production could by hauled away in a little more than seven hours working only three days a week. As a result, there were coal trucks from Rockford, Somonauk, Earlville, Serena, and Leland waiting to be loaded.

Besides playing cards and drinking coffee, there was little for the truckers to do in the meantime. Some of the truckers arranged saw horses and mattresses to get some sleep during the long delays, sometimes lasting 48 hours. Some drivers spent the weekend in the warm scale house in order to be first in line at the chutes on Monday morning, Feb. 27. One driver even came from Beaumont, Arkansas to comply with the "first come, first served" company policy. The only exceptions were shipments to those impoverished families on the list of Dee Bennett, the Poor Overseer, and to schools and hospitals.

Ottawa Mayor T. Berton Leamy did not release the exact terms of the emergency agreement with the Osage operators. Deliveries of the low-grade coal would be made to the Fred Scherer, Inc. coal yard. Gunner Scoog, said that there was also plenty of wood at the mine that could be picked up if people would provide their own means of transporting it. Anticipating the need for additional supplies, Berton also contacted the King and Hamilton Co. at 301 W. Marquette. They tried to place an order for a railroad carload of stoker coal. The two-day supply promised to the city of Ottawa from the Osage mine offered some relief for many local families whose coal bins were empty. It was common to see orders of upwards of 200 tons still waiting for their scheduled delivery.

City officials planned to establish a coal and wood station on Chestnut and Marquette Streets, where residents who claimed "emergency" situations, could purchase a small quantity of fuel. Supplies would be shipped to the station from Fred Scherer Inc. at 424 W. Madison, Lotts Lumber and Coal at 300 Joliet, and Bayne Coal Sales at 300 W. Marquette. As for wood supplies, the mayor was considering two locations about 14 miles southwest of Ottawa.

The dwindling supply of coal was having a significant impact on the Illinois Valley. On Feb. 25, Marquette Cement announced it was shutting down its Oglesby mill and laying off 200 men. On Monday, Feb. 27, Henry Zeliff announced the layoff of 200 men at Lehigh Portland Cement. The LaSalle News-Tribune reported that with Marquette operating only one of its ten kilns, the "cement industry was virtually paralyzed."

The abandoned Lehigh Cement silos and kilns in Oglesby stand as silent today as they did with the shutdown in February 1950. Photo by author.

The LaSalle County schools were operating on a shortened schedule. Classes only met from 8:30 a.m. until 12:30 p.m. to conserve what little coal remained for the boilers.

In eastern Bureau County, the Ladd Lumber and Coal Co. had completely sold out of its fuel stockpile. The Ladd

Elevator, which also handled coal, was also out. Sampsels and Day Foundry were operating on a four-day workweek.

The weather made the situation even more difficult. The temperature hovered around the zero mark at the Westclox weather station, and over five inches of snow blanketed the ground by the end of the week.

Strip-mining at the Osage mine reached 350-400 tons a day within a short time thanks to a separate UMW contract. By Feb. 28, the mine owners employed 16 union men.

The coal strike only seemed to get progressively worse for the ordinary citizens. On Mar. 2, an announcement appeared in the Bureau County Republican. The Illinois Allied Telephone Co. was closing on all Saturdays due to the coal crisis. The following day, while the Ottawa mayor and city officials were organizing emergency plans, the local papers reported eight coalmines in St. Clair County shut down.

Speaking for the UMW, Lewis still defended the strike claiming that there was enough coal on hand nationwide "if evenly distributed." That assurance did not deter local efforts to open the Ottawa coal and lumber station. James Hickey was in charge of the timber-cutting project on a lot north of Ottawa provided by T. L. Grot, who promised "free wood" to any resident who wanted to cut it on the 10-acre lot. Grot's only requirement was that those doing the cutting had to avoid damaging his property and clean up any debris. In a couple of days, 33 tons of wood were available at the Ottawa lumber station. Most of it was obtained from the Grot lot.

Since there was a limited supply of both wood and coal, the Ottawa Emergency Fuel Committee recommended another fuel, corncobs. Although local farmers would donate the cobs, residents would have to pay a fee to cover the trucking expenses.

In Wenona Mayor Ralph Goodwin appointed a committee consisting of John Garvin, Alfred Helander, and J.P. Manley to determine who would meet at the Wenona Coal Co. office every day. They would determine who would receive the limited supply of coal. The rationing policy was needed because the local supply was almost exhausted. One immediate impact was the cancellation of the Farmers Evening Classes in management and welding conducted by the agriculture department at Wenona H.S. The Farm Veteran School was moved from Monday evening to Monday afternoon.

Lee Carroll, head of the Ottawa fuel committee, drove to Springfield on Mar. 3 to apply for relief from the State Fuel Conservator in the Department of Mines and Minerals. He returned with the news that the state office was established to provide emergency fuel to hospitals and other "essential institutions" only, not for domestic shortages. The only other recourse for Ottawa was to submit an application to Governor Adlai Stevenson, who could request supplies from a federal or state emergency stockpile, such as the one located at Elwood.

A breakthrough in negotiations was finally reached on Mar. 4, when Lewis announced the UMW bargaining session had resulted in securing most but not all of the demands of the miners. He hoped that the mines could reopen on Mar. 6.

Lewis wasn't the only one looking forward to the return of the coal miners. John Messaglia, manager of the local Illinois Power plant, said the 25 percent dim-out authorized by the ICC would end immediately. Lee Carroll, speaking on behalf of the Ottawa Chamber of Commerce, announced the downtown streetlights, which had been shut off on Mar. 4, would be turned on again in the business district. Ottawa and Marquette high school students as well as all Ottawa public and parochial elementary school pupils were due back in the classrooms on Monday, Mar. 6.

In Spring Valley, the Immaculate Conception School and St. Bede Academy had not reopened. Lenten services, which had been cancelled in the Catholic churches, were back on schedule. Local industries went back to their previous work schedules. The emergency wood and fuel lot in Ottawa was closed as of Saturday night. The Rock Island trains that were suspended during the strike were expected to be running again on Saturday.

THE ROCK ISLAND RR TAKES CENTER STAGE

It seemed as though everything was back to normal again. The Rock Island trains were running again without incident until Mar. 30. The Republican Times described a major fire on the No. 502 Peoria *Rocket* just after it passed through Ottawa on the way to Chicago. The passenger train was traveling 90 mph as it approached Morris. Around 8 a.m., the wheels began to screech as the automatic braking system was activated. Train personnel directed passengers in the diner and coaches near the front of the train were to move to the rear coaches.

The train stopped only five miles west of Morris. Trainmen worked feverishly with hand-held extinguishers trying to halt the spreading flames under the diner. Volunteer firemen from Morris had a difficult time reaching the burning train because of muddy roads and the fact that the nearest grade crossing was 1,000 feet away from the train. The train crew was finally able to uncouple the burning cars, and a freight engine was brought to the scene where it was coupled to the burning cars and took them into Morris. A fire engine was waiting near the tracks in Morris, and the flames were finally extinguished.

Fortunately, the 200 passengers were out of harm's way. As soon as a steam engine was coupled to the undamaged cars, the passengers were able to continue their trip to Chicago arriving several hours late.

An inspection of the train revealed the cause of the fire. A pinion gear of a fuel pump had broken, and the part punctured the fuel tank. The fire gutted the diner and damaged the diesel.

The Rock Island RR was an integral part of the historic development of towns along its tracks. The following month, the long-awaited premier of "Rock Island Trail," caused a flurry of activity in Ottawa. While the Orpheum Theater in Ottawa would be the center of attention, businessmen used the event to assemble historic artifacts for window displays and placed numerous ads in the Republican Times to promote a variety of their products during the five-day event.

Ottawa officials planned an elaborate celebration. The Rock Island RR agreed to bring one of its old steam engines coupled to a tender and coach from Chicago to the Ottawa depot, where a delegation of city officials would greet the Rock Island RR dignitaries.

About 60 Ottawa businesses organized window displays, which focused on the history of their city in various ways. One display at Bell's Clothing Store was a collection of Indian artifacts and old guns used in buffalo hunting. These were donated for the occasion by Albert Hite of Dayton Township. Charles Bentzel, a worker on the Burlington RR, loaned his model railway equipment to the LaSalle Café. Residents could view an old picture of the

third county courthouse on display at the First National Bank. The Corbus Drug Store on LaSalle Street displayed photos of old Ottawa from the William Osman collection along with his old wet plate camera equipment. Among the unique displays was one at Adam's Drug Store. Visitors could see a traditional wooden Indian, which was once a common sight in front of nearly every cigar store. A collection of Indian artifacts was featured at the J.C. Penny store. The Block and Kuhl Clothing

Store displayed some typical post-Civil War women's attire of the period. Stiefel's Clothing Store on LaSalle Street filled their window with different photos of the store over the years, old household items, and even some of the wrapping paper they used in the 1870's. Mary E. Wilcox loaned her collection of table forks and an old rolling pin dating back to 1824 for the display at Shank's Clothing Store. Other businesses participating in the celebrations in various ways were Thumm's Furniture Co., the Gamble Store, Wagner's, Wallace Paint, Nina Antoine's Gift Shop, Herb Pyle Appliance Shop, Blackley Cleaners, Becker Drugs, and Rabenstein's.

Ads like this one and the one on the previous page from the Ottawa Republican Times were common in the weeks before the premiere of the "Rock Island Trail" movie at the Orpheum Theater.

At noon on Friday, April 28, Milton J. Formhals, president of the Chamber of Commerce, and John M. Jordan, president of Jordan's Hardware, met the train carrying James W. Hill and William E. Hayes, vice presidents of the railroad. From the depot, an automobile caravan brought the dignitaries to the Orpheum Theater. Ottawa mayor Leamy presented the Rock Island officials with the key to the city and then cut the ribbon marking the opening of the premiere.

The train carrying the Rock Island officials to Ottawa looked similar to this Rock Island train photographed in Peru. Maze Lumber photo.

A replica of the Rock Island depot in Ottawa was used as the setting for the movie version of the arrival of Abraham Lincoln for the Lincoln-Douglas debate. Senator Stephen Douglas did not take the train to Ottawa for the debate in 1858 but rather rode in a stagecoach from Peru. Photo by author.

Ottawa movie patrons were anxious to see their Rock Island depot in "Rock Island Trail." Ads like this one appeared for several days in the Republican Times. The movie was so well attended it was held over an extra day on Tuesday.

While the movie at the Orpheum Theater was a big draw, many other events were scheduled. On stage at the Orpheum, the Rock Island Rocket Chorus sang after each performance of the movie. On Saturday, there was a large crowd viewing the antiquated Rock Island steam engine, which returned to Chicago that evening.

On Monday evening at 9:15, Chief Walks-With-the-Wind, a Winnebago Indian from Starved Rock State Park, opened the program. Following his performance, throngs of people filled Jefferson Street in front of the Orpheum between LaSalle and Columbus Streets.

An estimated crowd of 3,000 were on hand to either watch or participate in a square dance contest. Ray Leach of Serena and Prudy Chapmen of Marseilles took turns calling the dance. Many of the dancers dressed in traditional western garb.

The Retail Merchants Association of the Chamber of Commerce awarded prizes consisting of silver dollars to individuals in several categories: the best-dressed couples, the youngest couple, the oldest individual, and the best circle of eight dancers. The Pitstick family won prizes for having the largest family participating in the dance. Eleven individuals split a total of $42 in silver cartwheels. It was a weekend long remembered by local residents.

THE TRAIN WAR

Just as things seemed to be quieting down again, another national strike gripped the Illinois Valley. This time, the American Federation of Labor Switchmen's Union walked off the job. Train service would be affected on the Rock Island, Western Pacific, Great Northern, Chicago Great Western, and the Denver and Rio Grande Western. Of these, the Rock Island RR covered the greatest distance – 8,000 miles of track.

The dispute had been brewing since April 19, when a presidential board made recommendations as to wages and hours for the union workers. The switchmen weren't alone in the dispute. The Brotherhood of Railroad Trainmen and the Order of Railway Conductors also rejected the board's proposals on June 15. Union leaders called the board findings "the most unjust, unfair, inequitable, and injurious report." One of the key demands of the switchmen was a reduction in the workweek to 40 hours from the standard 48 hours with no reduction in pay. They also wanted a raise of 31 cents an hour. While the government arbitrators were willing to concede the 40-hour workweek, the board only recommended an 18-cent raise.

The potential for a massive tie-up of the railroad system was ominous. About 21,000 miles of service on track from Chicago to the West Coast would be affected. In addition to the strikers, another 60,000 non-strikers would be idled. Even the Burlington RR would be affected since the trains used the Western Pacific RR tracks west of Salt Lake City.

The strike, which was anticipated to begin on Sunday, June 25, would require certain changes in Rock Island mail deliveries to LaSalle. To forestall any interruption in mail service, a mail truck was scheduled to leave Chicago at 5 a.m. and arrive at the LaSalle post office at 11 a.m. Mail from the west would be loaded into a second truck from Rock Island and be delivered in LaSalle at 10 a.m. All the parcel post and bulk mail would be carried by non-striking workers on the Burlington RR via Zearing.

As anticipated, the strike began on Sunday morning. The Great Northern RR was the only line of the four still running, but those trains were limited to passenger cars. No freight was moving on the GNRR. One immediate result in LaSalle was a significant increase in bus passengers traveling on three Santa Fe buses going to Chicago. The bus attendant also noted a "marked increase in passengers going to Peoria."

Growing hostilities on the Korean peninsula would soon demand an uninterrupted flow of war materials to the West Coast. However, those events in the Far East did not immediately have an impact on the strikers.

THE COLD WAR TURNS HOT

The Korean War did not begin as WWII did with a Pearl Harbor-type attack that mobilized the American people. The communist threat had become more intense after V-J Day. The Soviets shot down American planes and crews were lost when they probed Russia's coastal radar installations. Washington protested, but no serious reprisals were initiated. The military continued to focus on the threat of nuclear war with the Soviets.

When the North Koreans launched their attack across the 38th parallel, the stories made the front pages of the LaSalle and Ottawa newspapers. Initially, there were no banner headlines. Some senators in Washington even went out of their way to argue that the United States was under no obligation to go to war to defend the South Koreans. On June 26, President Truman took a more aggressive stand describing the invasion on June 24 as "unprovoked aggression," and he pledged the full support of the U.S. in the United Nations. The following day,

U.S. Air Force pilots were ordered to fly missions over South Korea. The American Pacific fleet was directed to protect Chaing Kai-shek's Formosa from possible Red Chinese invasion. The North Koreans quickly captured Seoul, the South Korean capital, even as America B-29 Superfortresses were bombing Kimpo airfield in the capital. The onslaught continued in the days that followed. On July 1, the American headquarters at Suwon, 20 miles south of Seoul was captured. In an action reminiscent of the WWII Doolittle Raid on Tokyo, 39 American bombers blasted the North Korean capital of Pyongyang.

In spite of the hostilities, there was no immediate call up of reservists by Secretary of Defense Louis Johnson. However, Truman did finally commit American ground forces in South Korea. The US Navy established a blockade around the peninsula. Locally, there seemed to be more interest in the problem of corn borers at the LaSalle County Farm Bureau. Fifty farmers met at Prairie Center at the end of June. Similar meetings were held in Grand Ridge, Lostant, and Seneca.

The gravity of the new conflict was simply not a priority concern in the Illinois Valley. However, that attitude began to change on July 1. The Defense Department issued orders barring visitors at all waterways, locks, and dams. Col. J. P. Campbell of the Chicago District Engineers said fences at the locks were being reinforced. Crews of towboats would not be allowed off their boats while passing through the locks at Marseilles and Starved Rock, and there would be no delivery of supplies to the boats. With the exception of those on official government business, all visitors were barred at the local locks.

Such actions in the Illinois Valley increased awareness of the potential seriousness of the conflict. However, even Gen. MacArthur downplayed the possibility of another major conflict. In his report to the Pentagon on July 6, he advised the decision makers the fighting was "not considered serious in any way." The Air Force had knocked out 8 North Korean tanks and 45 trucks as they drove 60 miles south of the capital chasing the retreating South Korean and American forces.

The Starved Rock Locks were "off limits" during the Korean War. After 9/11, certain photography was prohibited at the Marseilles and Starved Rock Locks. Photo by author.

USAF photo of a flight of B-29s over North Korea. For security reasons, bomber crews could not write home about their missions.

The reality of the fighting in Korea began to be taken to heart when the names of the first casualties were reported. On July 4, Cpl. Ray Morrissey, son of Charolotte Morrissey of Bloomington, was reported as one of the missing men in a flight from Japan to Korea.

Soon, more reports about the action in the Far East of local interest began to fill the newspapers. R.J. Comisky, who attended Lostant and L-P high schools, was sent to Korea in a civilian capacity for the Economic Cooperation Administration. He arrived in Korea and was in the American Embassy in Seoul when the war broke out. Comisky, whose parents, Mr. and Mrs. Richard Comisky resided on a farm in rural Lostant, described his experience to an AP reporter. "We thought it was just another border skirmish until we heard the gunfire."

Americans were evacuated as quickly as possible. Comisky boarded an Air Force C-46, and while he couldn't see any actual fighting, he could hear it in the distance. He was joined by men, women, and children during the orderly departure. The evacuees were flown to an undisclosed location in Japan. The young man from Lostant had to wait eight days in Tokyo before being sent back to the states on a chartered plane by way of Shemya, Alaska, where they were delayed for 18 hours because of the weather. When he arrived in Seattle, he was surprised at the reaction of American civilians. Based on what he had heard on the radio, he felt that there was far less concern in Japan than in the United States. "The people here seem more jittery," he said.

Indeed, Americans were more anxious. Local communities appeared to be returning to their WWII experiences. In Marseilles, an emergency air defense plan was set up for the city. Harold Fewell was selected as project chairman to coordinate dim-outs and blackouts. An aircraft observation center was also established. The centers, under the command of the USAF, would be located every eight miles.

In Ottawa, civil defense officer Alex Bower, announced the names of 20 men who were selected to serve on the Air Raid Warning Service Board, which worked in conjunction with the U.S. Army. The Eastern Aerial Defense Corps picked Bower to head the board. The observation post located on the roof of the Bower Brake Co. would be manned 24 hours a day. The Ottawa air raid wardens were John Gage, Herbert H. Beguin, Carl Weishast, George Andrews, J. Ogden

Andrews, Oliver M. Orres, Joe Armstrong, Howard Boe, John Corcoran, Leroy Hutchinson, Glenn Harris, Dominic Consalvo, Ray Shumaker, Thomas Bower, Ernest Melland, Martin Oslani, Earl L. Olson, Howard Brockman, Loran Defenbaugh, and John Daugherty.

Civilian volunteers were needed on the home front just as they were in WWII, but young men were also needed to fill in the ranks of the armed forces. After demobilization, the Army was down to eleven divisions, only four of which were in the Far East. On July 7, Truman authorized the Pentagon to draft men. Seeking to avoid the use of a draft to increase the size of the armed forces, one unnamed army official said, "If (reserve) strengths are met without the use of Selective Service, we will be very happy."

Truman also decided that the continuing strike on the Rock Island was a threat to national security so he seized the railroad and authorized the army to run the trains for the government. The Rock Island depot manager in Ottawa, R.A. Lynch, responded to the presidential action by saying that at least one Rock Island freight train was expected to run through Ottawa on July 8, In his opinion, however, there would be no passenger service. The workers were still striking for a 31-cent hourly raise and a 40-hour workweek. Truman's announcement called on the railroad men to return to work under their previous contract while negotiations were underway.

Finally, on July 10, a court order forced the switchmen back to their jobs. Arthur Glover, president of the switchmen's union said, "We have no choice now." A Rock Island freight train came through Ottawa on Saturday night, and the No. 502 Peoria Rocket passenger train stopped at the depot on Sunday morning. At least there was a truce in the railroad war.

Meanwhile in Ottawa, a draft office was established to handle the Washington requirements for troops. Charles Gapen headed the draft board. He was assisted by R. C. Woodford and Robert Illiff of Ottawa; and Robert Young of Marseilles. The Illinois statewide draft quota was initially set at 1,200 men. Of that number, 569 men would be selected from downstate.

Small towns like Granville also established draft boards to fill the government draft quotas. An office was opened on the second floor of the Trahd building at McCoy and Harrison. It was open only on Fridays and staffed by Miss June Younger of Lostant, who was responsible for the clerical work for Putnam, Marshall, and Stark counties. The local board members were drawn from four towns: Conrad Bickerman, Magnolia; Art Wilson, McNabb; Steve Novak, Hennepin; and Stan Treudt, Granville.

More men were being recruited for the National Guard unit from the Ottawa area. Vacancies in two companies were being filled at the Ottawa armory at 201 East Main St. One of the benefits of joining one of the units was the automatic deferment for young men 19 to 26 years old. They would not be subject to the Army draft. That policy did not seem to prevent Illinois from filling its quota for the draft. In July 1950, there was still a pool of 90,000 men, who were classified A-1 and eligible for the draft. Hostilities in South Korea were becoming intense, and many young men would be called by local draft boards to report for induction.

The North Koreans were using Russian tanks to drive the Americans back to the Kum River. In one brutal attack, the communists were able to infiltrate American lines at night by wearing civilian clothes. MacArthur put a positive spin on the attack reporting, "The armed forces are continuing their action to stabilize the North Korean offensive about the Kum River."

The Times published one of the firsthand reports of the combat from Cpl. Carl T. Formhals, 20, whose parents lived on Locust Street in South Ottawa. He was with a small group of soldiers trapped behind enemy lines for six days. They were cut off from their unit when they were attacked by a line of 30 tanks. One of the men in the group, Pvt. James Gibson of Panama City, FL, said that they were only separated from the pursuing Reds by a ridgeline at times. The group lost one of their men in a firefight while crossing an open rice paddy. South Korean soldiers helped Formhals and three other men to get back to the American lines.

The pace of reports of local men fighting in Korea began to pick up. One of the men from Peru, Lt. C.F. Hybki, wrote his parents, Mr. and Mrs. Casimir Hybki Sr., who shared the information with the News-Tribune. During the first week of the fighting, he said he had flown four combat missions in his B-17 rescue plane over enemy territory. In the bomb bay, the aircraft carried a 30-foot motorized boat, which could be dropped to rescue any crews that ditched in the sea. His bomber also had a full compliment of machine gunners, who successfully drove off enemy fighter planes on their second sortie from their base at Ashya air base on Kyushu.

The battles raged on in Korea with the accompanying result of more American casualties. At the end of July, the News-Tribune reported that Cpl. Robert Van Natta of Amboy had been wounded, but no details were available.

LaSalle Draft Board 152, chaired by Herman Frederick, sent out orders for 80 men to take their pre-induction physicals between August 17 and Aug. 21. It was the second big call-up in a week. In early September, Ottawa Draft Board 153, which included Ottawa and areas south of the Illinois River, ordered 54 men to take their physicals in Chicago. Twenty-one of the men were from Streator, and 17 lived in Ottawa. Smaller towns had correspondingly smaller quota: three from Oglesby, two each from Tonica and Wenona, and one each from Dana and Ransom.

The North Koreans were scoring one victory after another. They rolled across the Naktong River and captured Pohang on the east coast of the peninsula.

In spite of Truman's assertions that there were large stockpiles of material to supply the military, a new government agency, the National Production Authority (NPA), began to list those materials needed for the war effort. Eleven items – aluminum, cement, copper, lead, leather, lumber, paper, synthetic and natural rubber, steel, wool, and zinc – were identified as necessary war materials. However, rationing on a local level, as in WWII, was not yet imposed on the civilians.

Trying to curb the WWII memories of OPA rationing, Washington insisted that there was no prospect of food shortages and the practice of hoarding was foolish. According to government reports, there were tremendous stockpiles of wheat, corn, and cotton; a bumper harvest was forecast.

Although Truman insisted that rationing would not be necessary, the local papers carried ads reminding people of the shortages in the previous conflict. This ad appeared in the July 14, 1950 edition of the News-Tribune.

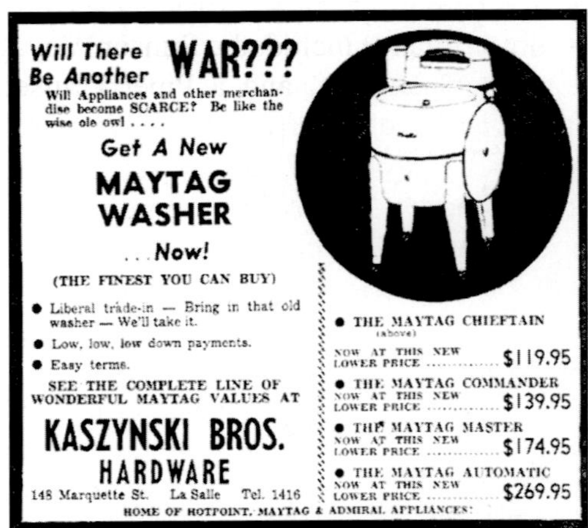

Recognizing the need for home front preparedness in the event of another world conflict, the Red Cross director of disaster service met with representatives from Marshall County on Aug. 14 in Lacon. Max Rote, the speaker at the meeting, requested the civic organizations in Wenona and the other cities in the county to determine the number of public buildings that would be "suitable for mass shelter or feeding or both which would be available in case of emergency." Meetings like this were being conducted at the 47 Red Cross chapters across northern Illinois to prepare for any national crisis.

The theme of preparedness was reflected a few weeks later when the first civilian fly-in was conducted at Chanute Field near Rantoul. George Braymen, the Wenona supervisor of the Ground Observer Corps, Burdette Evans, Bernard Flahaven, Frank Kinsey, and Robert Burgess represented Wenona in the meeting. Gen. B. E. Gates, the base commander, addressed the 350 pilots stressing their role as "one of the bulwarks of our defense." Later, the pilots viewed the B-29's, B-36's, B-50's and various other planes at Chanute.

Wenona was noted for having ' more active pilots and planes per population than any other town in Illinois" according to the Wenona Index. Fourteen individuals were student pilots awaiting certification as pilots. The assemblage of private planes included a Stinson Voyager, a Globe Swift, an Aeronca Champion, and a Piper Cruiser. Three more planes were expected to arrive at the Wenona airport, two Boeing Stearman bi-planes and a Grumman Navy Wildcat fighter.

While civilians on the home front prepared in small ways for a possible crisis, the conflict in Korea became a more troubling reality for some families. Occasionally, a letter appeared in the newspaper describing the fighting. Mr. and Mrs. John Hall of Troy Grove had encouraging news from their son Jack, a Pfc. in Co. A of the 9th Infantry Regiment. In his two-week old correspondence, the young private told how he was in a foxhole with his automatic rifle sitting under a hot sun with only a piece of a pup tent to shade him. His unit had been fighting the "gooks," as he called the North Koreans, for twelve days. With the arrival of the Marines, they were finally able to cross a river. The enemy forces were driven back with 1,000 dead; their bodies covered the riverbank. Hall closed his letter saying, "I will sure be glad when this is over."

For other families, the news was more disheartening. Mr. and Mrs. Ernest Galli of Naplate learned their son, Sgt. 1/c Armand Galli, was wounded by a sniper on Aug. 13 while on patrol. Unlike most of the men in Co. F of the 9th Infantry, he was a veteran having seen action at Normandy and in the Battle of the Bulge in WWII and serving with the Allied occupation forces in Austria after the war. Galli recovered and was sent back into the lines only to be killed at Yongsan, South Korea on Sept. 1.

Three local families waited anxiously after learning that their sons, Cpl. Carl Pitts of Marseilles, Pvt. Russell Ham of Ottawa, and Pfc. Stanley Samolinski of LaSalle were missing in action. Mr. and Mrs. John Samolinski of 560

Blackstone, LaSalle, were informed that their son, Pfc. Stanley Samolinski, of the 29th Infantry Combat Regiment was killed in action near Hadong on July 27. He was the first soldier from LaSalle County killed in the fighting.

Pfc. Samolinski photo from the News-Tribune, Sept. 14, 1950.

Other families received distressing letters from the Defense Department. Pvt. Warren J. Feldges, 18, from Tiskilwa died from his wounds at the Chindong-ni Schoolhouse on Aug. 3. Another man from Bureau County, Cpl. Joe Cieslak, was killed. Sgt. Charles Hewitt of Princeton was wounded on Aug. 2 and returned to duty. He was later killed while serving as a scout with a 5th Cavalry regiment behind enemy lines on Oct. 3. One of Streator's WWII veterans, Cpl. Walter D. Rowatt, 42, already had 20 years of military service and was ready to retire in a few months. He was killed in action while fighting with the 64th Field Artillery battery on Sept. 3. His brother, William, of 710 East Broadway, Streator received the notification from the Defense Department stating that he had died from his wounds. No specific details of his brother's death were included.

September 1950 marked a turning point in the communist aggression. The landings at Inchon, South Korea and the breakout from the 120-mile front around Pusan turned the tide. Marines captured the Kimpo Airfield, which was located 12 miles northeast of Inchon.

The war continued to take its toll of men from the Illinois Valley. Robert Smith of Marseilles, Ralph Atherton of

Meriden, Harold M. Collins of Seneca, and Pfc. Dale Shirey of Mendota were names added to the casualty lists. Cpl. Horace B. Bartlett, Jr. of Seneca was killed on Sept. 18 at Taegu, and Pfc. Albert F. Leslie of Streator with the 7th Cavalry Regiment of the 1st Cav. Division was killed in action on Sept. 20.
Pfc. Leslie photo from Korean War Project.

Increasing casualties resulted in a call-up of reservists. William Ohlendorf Jr. was the first called from Utica. He had already served in WWII in the South Pacific and with Patton's 3rd Army in Europe was required to report to Camp Hood, TX.

Several men from LaSalle County were killed in the early days of fighting. Pfc. Ralph Salvati from Streator lost his life on Sept. 28 while assigned to the 2nd Engineer Combat Battalion 2nd Inf. Div. in South Korea. Pfc. Ralph Salvati photo from Korean War Project.

Pfc. Samuel K. Meagher from Seneca was serving in the 2nd Division when he was initially reported as MIA. The record was revised. He was listed as killed in the fighting around Kunu-ri, North Korea on Dec. 1.

On Sept. 28, Putnam County residents read that Pfc. Melvin Liles was wounded. It took over two weeks for the reports of his injuries to reach his parents, Mr. and Mrs. Floyd Liles of Granville. Liles had reenlisted in 1947 after having served five years in WWII. He became the first Putnam County casualty in the Korean fighting.

There were others from the Putnam County in harm's way. Pfc. Clair Bishop from Mark and Cpl. Melvin Greathouse from Granville were also serving in Korea. Veterans, including Capt. Bud Donaldson and Bill Forney, were ordered to report for duty.

On Oct. 6, Truman signed a proclamation ordering the drafting of doctors and dentists. In LaSalle County all eligible doctors, veterinarians, and dentists were notified to report to the Ottawa draft office at 606 Court St. This included all those under age 50, who were not in the reserves or who had actively served in the military. Those drafted faced a tour of duty of 21 months. There was a way to avoid the draft; doctors could volunteer and receive a monthly bonus of $100. The army needed 300 medical doctors by Nov. 15, and 300 dentists and 50 veterinarians by Dec. 15. The draft was only for the army; the navy and air force did not need to draft doctors or dentists.

Capt. Ray Guisti from Mark was already serving with the army medical corps in Korea. His descriptions of the combat area added realism to the fighting on the other side of the world. Doctor Guisti was billeted in a small schoolhouse with rain pouring through the blown out windows. In a letter from Inchon dated Sept. 26, he wrote, "The town is almost leveled and the people have that dazed look of bewilderment, wondering what it's all about." He went on to describe the children who were foraging for something to eat "like hungry animals" while older people were digging in the ruins.

Weeks later, another of Dr. Guisti's letters, dated Oct 4, appeared in the Oct 19 issue of the Putnam County Record. His company took over a schoolhouse in Seoul and began to convert it into a hospital. It was a dangerous situation since there were still snipers and machine gunners in the sector. He wrote, "(Seoul) is about 80 percent destroyed. The capitol was still burning, bodies were strewn all over the streets, and I almost cried when I saw the bodies of innocent children piled up like so many pieces of wood."

Dr. Guisti (pictured) told his parents how the Korean mountains covered the landscape. He pointed out the irony of the names of the mountains, such as Mountain of Lasting Peace and the Hill of Joy, in a war-torn country.

For one week, Dr. Guisti had worked with the graves registration corps to determine the cause of death of the American soldiers. "They were atrocity victims," he said.

Working with others, they organized a makeshift hospital in a Korean school to make room for civilian casualties. Within half a day, they were treating civilians and performing surgery. Their day began at 6 a.m. and continued into the evening hours when surgical operations were performed.

The Korean people, Guisti wrote, had little to eat. Those with a little money might have a bowl of rice while the poor ate only millet or barley. They added a radish to the meals with a piece of fish. Rather than tea, the impoverished Koreans drank rice water with "infusions of sugar and orange peels." The Americans weren't allowed to eat the local food because of the surface sewer system. Diseases, such as dysentery, cholera, and smallpox were epidemic. Guisti closed his letter telling his parents he was in good health except for the bites from lice in his sleeping bag.

While stationed at Suwon airfield south of Seoul, Guisti's unit came under attack from an enemy pilot they called "Bedtime Charlie." He flew over the base with some regularity and dropped a bomb. The medical personnel dove for cover when an alert was sounded. These incidents might remind M*A*S*H television fans of the episode first aired on Sept. 22, 1973, when "Five O'Clock Charlie" flew over the unit attempting to bomb an ammo dump Instead of Hawkeye Pierce and Trapper John watching the North Korean, in reality it could have been Doctor Guisti from Mark, IL and a nurse who took cover under a truck while the field was bombed.

Guisti was transferred back to Pusan harbor, where he wrote home in late October while aboard the troopship USNS *General Greely*. "If MacArthur's prediction comes true (war over in a few days) we may be scratched, if not you'll know we sailed for ports on the northeast coast near Manchuria."

Doctor Guisti was one of the military personnel aboard the USNS *General Greely*, a troop transport ship used in the Korean War. Official US Navy photo.

        While in the Pusan area, Doctor Guisti was billeted at a Swedish hospital with about 160 volunteer officers, doctors, nurses, and enlisted men under the jurisdiction of the Swedish Red Cross. He commented in his letter to his parents in Mark how the Swedish doctors had to bring their own instruments or pick some up from the Americans.

        News of the war continued to make front-page stories in local papers. Another casualty from Peru was Cpl. Wayne Potthoff, 20, who was suffering from a concussion received when a North Korean shell exploded near him. The former captain of the L-P frosh-soph football team enlisted in the Marines and was assigned to the 7th Regiment of the First Marine Division. When he wrote to his sister, Mrs. Lucille Doll in LaSalle, he was recovering in a navy hospital in Japan.

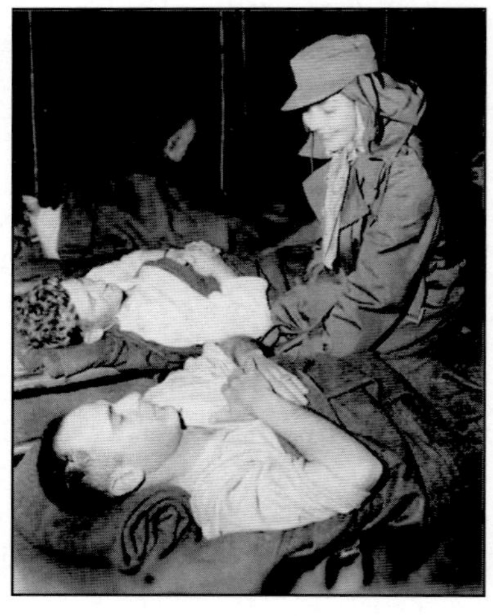

One of the uplifting occasions of the war was the arrival of USO entertainers. In addition to Bob Hope's group there was a visit by Hollywood actress Jennifer Jones, who was nominated for several Academy Awards in the 1940's. Photo by Capt. Ray Guisti.

        USO shows brought some relief to the tension of war, and the soldiers appreciated the generosity of the Hollywood personalities who entertained them close to the front. So, it was disturbing for Illinois Valley residents to read in the News-Tribune that Hollywood actor, Al Jolson, 64, died. He had just returned from performing for the troops in Korea just as he had done in WWII. Best known for his role in the 1927 film, "The Jazz Singer," he was scheduled to record a radio broadcast on the Bing Crosby show before his untimely death.

Not all major stories focused on the fighting overseas. Many local history buffs were interested in seeing the Illinois Central's "Lincoln Train" that was scheduled to stop in LaSalle Oct. 28-29. This would be an unique opportunity to view over 60 relics from Lincoln's childhood to his assassination for two days in a railway car located on an IC siding at the east end of First St. LaSalle was to be one of the IC's last stops in Illinois.

A story of national significance was the attempted assassination of President Truman by Puerto Rican nationalists. The event occurred on Nov. 1 at Blair House near the White House. During the fusillade of shooting, three White House guards were shot; most of the would-be assassins were killed. One of the attackers, who survived his wounds, was later tried; found guilty; and sentenced to death.

WOULD AMERICA BE ATTACKED?

Although the fighting in Korea seemed to be less intense, there were still concerns of a possible Russian bomber attack on the Illinois Valley. The 8,500 civil defense observers scattered across the country, in conjunction with the USAF, were involved in a nationwide weekend drill in November.

In Wenona, an air defense center was established on the roof of the Goodwin Brothers Garage (pictured). One early November weekend, 23 volunteers participated in a practice exercise to report on any

military, commercial, or private aircraft flying in the area. Supervisor George Braymen, and chief observers Oral Axline, Everett Nelson, Ronald Tallyn, Chester Kunze, and Willard Stewart, directed the activity. Volunteers worked one-hour shifts from 9 a.m. until 6 p.m. for two days and reported 15 aircraft to the Air Force interceptor command. Wenona became one of the 300 posts in the Midwest in the GOC.

In Ottawa 23 observers worked in shifts during the exercise at the Bower Brake and Electric Co. building at 601 W. Norris Dr. Any record of "enemy" planes (those not known to be from the Ottawa area) would be immediately called in to the Chicago filter center, which would determine if the planes were friend or foe. The main reason the Air Force was counting on the use of visual observers was that radar was not too effective against low flying planes. The civilian observers would supplement the radar stations.

Some individuals felt there were other dangers besides "enemy planes" flying over the Illinois Valley. A presentation on the spreading threat of communism in America was scheduled at LaSalle-Peru H.S. for Nov. 4. Senator Joseph McCarthy (pictured) spoke to a capacity audience in the school auditorium about the "pinks" and "reds" as they infiltrated the State Department and  affected the U.S. foreign policy. McCarthy developed a reputation for targeting prominent government officials as communists or sympathizers of the communist agenda.

While McCarthy was describing the need to battle communism in America, the real fight continued overseas. During the weeks before Thanksgiving, the American and South Korean troops had crossed the 38th parallel; captured the North Korean capital, Pyongyang; and drove the Communists back to the Yalu River, the border with Communist China. Gen. MacArthur was so confident of a quick end to the war he inspected the enemy positions from his personal plane 60 miles behind enemy lines at the Yalu River.

MacArthur's conclusions were overly optimistic. The following week, a force of 20,000 Chinese counterattacked and during two days of fighting, advanced 12-20 miles. On Nov. 28, the News-Tribune headline read, "UN Faces Entirely New War." Soon, 27 enemy divisions were pouring across the Yalu

River. The Chinese army attacking the UN forces even included 8,000-14,000 Mongolian cavalrymen mounted on small ponies and accompanied by supply caravans of camels. The UN forces in the west, including most of the 8th Army, retreated to the 38th parallel. Those in the northeast fought their way to the port of Hungnam, where a fleet of UN ships was ready to evacuate them.

One of the American pilots flying mercy missions during the December fighting was Lt. Ken Dudgeon of Ottawa. The former WWII pilot was assigned to the 437th Troop Carrier Wing. On one of Dudgeon's flights, they loaded his C-46 with a platoon of battered Marines, who had fought a 76-hour battle with the Chinese. Mortar shells exploded near Dudgeon's C-46 during the takeoff. It was a bumpy ride for the wounded Marines, many of whom suffered severe frostbite. When they landed, the Marines thanked the crew for getting them back to a safe location.

USAF photo of a C-46 cargo plane, the type piloted by Lt. Dudgeon in Korea.

LST's line the beachhead at Hungnam evacuating American troops. US Navy photo.

One of those Marines who experienced the horrible weather and human wave attacks of the Chinese was Ron Sarles, son of Mr. and Mrs. Roscoe Sarles of 1611 Kansas St. in Ottawa. He was among 600 Marines, who were attacked by an estimated force of 22,000 Chinese. In a letter to his parents, Sarles wrote about the Chinese attack for five days and nights. The Marines held on, destroying the entire Chinese force. He said the temperature in the mountains dropped to 20-30 degrees below zero causing widespread frostbite. He suffered a couple of frozen toes himself but was otherwise in good health. Sarles and his fellow Marines made it back to Hungnam, where they were transported back to Japan to regroup.

Another story of the fighting came with a phone call to Ruth Lee Atherton in LaSalle from her son, George Atherton, a sailor aboard the destroyer USS *Mansfield*. The dangers were different for naval vessels off the coast of Korea. In November, the *Mansfield* struck a floating mine, injuring 23 sailors. The side of the ship was badly damaged, and the vessel had to be towed into the port. Although Atherton was not injured, it was the second time he was aboard a ship in Korean waters that had struck mines.

US Navy photo of DD 728 USS *Mansfield* during the Korean War.

A few days later, the local papers reported on the heavy casualties some units experienced. Cpl. Robert Hamil wrote to his parents, Mr. and Mrs. William Hamil at 1620 Champlain St., Ottawa, about his survival in a battle that virtually wiped out his entire battalion. From Hamhung, North Korea he wrote, "I guess I was just lucky, mom, as it was hell. I have seen the result of war and hope I never have to see it again. We lost our whole battalion except for a few men." Reassigned as a mail clerk in Hamhung, northeast of the evacuation port of Hungnam, he said, "We have one tent full of mail that will never be given to those whom it was meant for. It will be sent back home. The worst is over for me and I'm just as good as ever-just a little nervous."

Battles resulted in many casualties such as Pfc. William Baker, a 19-year old from Seneca. His parents received word of his recovery in a hospital in Osaka, Japan. He was recovering from the shrapnel wounds he received while fighting in North Korea. Almost two dozen men from Bureau, Lee, Grundy, Marshall, and LaSalle counties were killed in the fighting in 1950.

Several local men, such as Marine Sgt. Frederick Eubler of Streator, were decorated for unusual bravery. He came under heavy fire while stringing telephone wires near Yongsan. He was the first soldier from Streator to be awarded the Silver Star medal in Korea. Roy C. Johnson of Freedom Township was also awarded the same medal for bravery under fire and was given a field promotion to Staff Sergeant.

Concerns of a wider war involving the Soviets prompted authorities to expand civil defense preparations. The Rock Island Air Raid Warning Area included the entire northwestern area of Illinois. In December, the state director sent instructions to Bureau, LaSalle, Marshall, Putnam, Lee, Knox, Stark, Fulton, Tazewell, and other counties in the area. The area director wrote to the Princeton unit, "It is unlikely Princeton would be subjected to such an (atomic bomb) attack, but it will have to play an important role in Civil Defense." There was a need to train local volunteers against an atomic bomb blast and to prepare against sabotage of communication, transportation, and manufacturing facilities. He suggested the

Princeton, Peru, LaSalle, and Ottawa resources might be combined in a coordinated plan.

Bureau County took the threat of a nuclear attack seriously. The local Red Cross chapter scheduled a first aid course at Princeton H.S. and hoped to enroll every adult to care for refugees who might be transferred from bombed cities. An advisory council was formed consisting of Melvin May, Forrest Booth, Dr. John Maloney, Arnold Walter, W.C. Duffield, Cliff Thompson, Harvey Nieman, Leo Evelhoch and Carl Huitine. A first aid and nursing program was organized by the Bureau County Red Cross to provide assistance to the local civil defense unit. The goal was to train one of every eight adults.

THE WAR ON GAMBLING

Meanwhile, a different type of battle was being waged in the Illinois Valley. For decades, illegal gambling was common in Illinois. Some looked at the activity as a harmless form of entertainment while others felt it was an evil that had to be eliminated. In Bureau and LaSalle counties, roulette, slot machines, punchboards, and similar gaming devices were commonplace and had been moneymakers for taverns and casinos for decades. However, during the 1950's, there was a serious effort to eliminate gambling across the state.

Ironically, 1950 started with the hijacking of the one-armed bandits at locations in Cedar Point and LaSalle. Three robbers had been stealing the machines from various locations for a month. Joe Cherri's and Mary's taverns were hit in mid-January, but there was no record of the theft reported to the sheriff in Ottawa, and the Cedar Point mayor, Leonard Reed, said he didn't know anything about the thefts.

Small scale operations were nothing compared to the illegal gambling found in and around LaSalle County. The work of an undercover reporter from Chicago, Martin O'Connor (right), during the fall of 1949 was revealed to the public in a series of News-Tribune articles beginning on Jan. 31, 1950.

Arriving in the city at the Rock Island depot in the fall of 1949, O'Connor hailed a Yellow cab and sought some "action." He soon discovered that there were crap games within 10 minutes of the railroad station, and it was only a 15-minute cab ride from downtown to a brothel. He was also introduced at one tavern to the lucky bowls seen in many of the bars. He found out his first night in town how easy it was to lose $12 in less than a half hour. O'Connor was really after one of the biggest operations in LaSalle. Kelly and Cawley's casino at 621 First St. There he would find a bookie, slots, baseball betting, lucky bowls, punchboards, roulette, and crap tables. There was gambling also going on at Jimmy Kays, Duffy's tavern, Saratoga at 504 First, the Senate at 517 First St. the El Mirador in the Hotel Francis, and the Silver Congo at 559 First. He also found that there were crap games going on across the river in Oglesby at the Diamond Horseshoe and at South Bluff Country Club. Everything was wide open and easy to observe.

South Bluff country club has changed very little since the 1950's. Photo by author.

Tom Cawley, the proprietor of Kelly and Cawley's offered his customers more than gambling. The establishment also included a dining room, bar, and musical entertainment. For those who wanted to gamble, there was something for everyone at the two-floor casino, a bingo parlor and roulette for the ladies; poker and craps for the men. Thirty slot machines sucked in the nickels, dimes, and quarters. Cawley bragged that no one could ever beat him in the long run and told the story of one young man who one night won a $1,000 and lost $1,600 the next night. The craps odds always favored the house $1.40 to $1.00. Cawley also had a monopoly on horse betting. Bettors at the Paddock in Streator learned the race results as they were phoned in from LaSalle. O'Connor concluded that Cawley had to do business with the gangs in Chicago because they had partial or total control over the race wire services. The Bell Telephone Co. could remove the phone lines if someone complained the phones were being used for illegal purposes.

However, State's Attorney Charles Helfrich never filed a complaint in spite of numerous tips that there was book making at Cawley's. Without such a complaint, nothing could be done to stop the practice.

Casinos and taverns lined First Street in LaSalle. Looking east on First Street at the intersection with Gooding St. was the Silver Congo casino. Across the street on the NE corner was Duffy's tavern. A few doors further east was Kelly and Cawley's at 621 First Street. On the south side of the street was another tavern and gambling center, the Rose Bowl. Ryan Cawley photo collection.

O'Connor could not help but note the lack of law enforcement on the part of the LaSalle police department. He wrote in his Feb. 14 article, "On a warm day, the noise of the bookie is loud enough to be heard outside." He accused the police of wearing blinders and had cotton in their ears. They had their orders – seldom, if ever, to interfere with Tom Cawley.

According to reporter Tom O'Connor, LaSalle mayor Matt Bildhauer didn't know there was gambling in his city.

Meanwhile, the book on the second floor, located between the dining room and the crap room, continued to open promptly at noon for the "morning line," a daily description of the names of the horses, their jockeys, odds, and the starting time of each race. O'Connor continued his investigation, playing the various games. On one occasion, he did well and cashed out his slip from the eye-in-the-sky for $55.

Walter Green, a former state trooper, was one of the "eyes" employed by Tom Cawley. His job was to watch the action at the craps and roulette tables to catch would-be "sharpers," gamblers, who might try to slip some loaded dice into the game. Photo from Dorothy Cusick collection.

If one of the "eyes" spotted someone cheating, the individual was promptly thrown out of the club. There was also the occasional sneak thief who would try to grab some uncollected bet on a payoff from the dealer. A lucky craps shooter was given a payoff ticket by the "eye." The tickets were then redeemed at the cashier's cage located on the south side of the crap's room. Even the losers tended to come back for more action the next week.

The undercover reporter finally had a personal meeting with Cawley on Oct. 20, 1949. The outcome of that brief encounter was revealed in the LaSalle paper on Feb. 21, 1950.

Cawley claimed, "Somebody around here is a stool pigeon and we don't know who it is." Referring to leaks to the News-Tribune, Cawley told O'Connor, "We have several people in mind, but we can't pin it on you or anyone else." Cawley, who was gazing at the ceiling as he spoke, finally leaned forward and spoke directly, "O'Connor, I don't want to see you get hurt, and you know how I operate."

The reporter tried to call the gambling czar's bluff saying, "I am not going to be hurt by you or anyone else." However, he knew that the tired businessman was serious. "You want me to stay away from your crap table, is that it?" Cawley answered directly, "That is right."

The masquerade was over for the reporter. He knew Cawley had found his man so he tried to end the encounter with an amicable gesture. "I will give you my word that I will not gamble in here any more. If I do gamble in here, I will tell you in advance. That is the best I can do for you." O'Connor would continue his investigation to document the widespread gambling in the town that became known as "Little Reno."

O'Connor was supposed to file another gambling story the following week. His next target was the Diamond Horseshoe in Oglesby. Unexpectedly, the owner, Leo Kautz, was brought to trial for operating a gambling establishment; paid his fine; and closed his nightclub.

The Diamond Horseshoe was a popular nightclub offering music, dancing, drinking, and gambling. Dorothy Debosik collection.

Justice did not always progress swiftly in LaSalle County. In February, charges were finally brought against 13 gambling establishments that were raided in September 1949 by Chief Kasprowicz. Fines were levied against the accused, but eight of the defendants sought an appeal and jury trials. It would not be until April 1950 that the issue was settled when 11 of the defendants, Tom Cawley, William "Tinney" Cosgrove, owner of the Silver Congo, and nine other tavern and restaurant owners, pleaded guilty of the lesser charge of disorderly conduct instead of possession of gambling devices, which would have cost them their liquor licenses. Judge John Massieson fined each owner $100 and costs.

The Paddock (pictured at left center) at 116 E. Main St. in Streator, opened in 1939. It was one of the main restaurants and gambling establishments in Streator. About 38 people worked there. The Paddock didn't have a wire to get the race results so the club bookie called Cawley's in LaSalle to record the winning horses. The business was licensed to Lloyd D. Johnson, but it was generally known that Tom Cawley was the real operator. Streator Historical Society photo.

Meanwhile in Bureau County, deputies raided three taverns in the village of Ohio but only found a small number of punchboards and some lottery tickets. The Harry Etheridge tavern was given a "clean bill" by the raiders. Nonetheless, it was well known that gambling was "flourishing in the south and western sections of the county" according to the News-Tribune.

In early March, Illinois Attorney General Ivan Elliott began putting pressure on Helfrich claiming the local state's attorney could stop the gambling if he wanted to. "If a man can not clean his house there is always a chance of someone cleaning it for him," Elliott suggested.

With Elliott's claim that the LaSalle gambling situation was the "worst in the state" ringing in his ears, Helfrich finally took action. He sent a letter to Sheriff Ed Ryan and Mayor Bildhauer. Essentially, the state's attorney said that all gambling must stop in LaSalle County. The threat resulted in a temporary clean up of the LaSalle gambling activities. By May, there was no sign of gambling even at the Paddock in Streator and Kelly and Cawley's.

The statewide gambling cleanup ordered by Gov. Stevenson also produced results in the Morris area. In late May, 100 state police officers raided over 100 gaming locations and seized 182 slot machines valued at $60,000 in a sweep through Jo Davies, Grundy, and Iroquois counties.

The most significant haul in Grundy County was made at the Seven Gables Inn on Rt. 6 near Morris. Inside they found 31 slot machines, two dice tables, a roulette wheel and a blackjack table all in operation. The building even had a back room where the slot machines, even those from other gambling establishments, were repaired. Frank Black, the father of Grundy County's State's Attorney August B. Black, was among those charged with operating a bookmaking establishment.

In Bureau County, Princeton Police Chief Cliff Thompson said, "There is no gambling here." News-Tribune investigators agreed with that assessment in June. A raid by the chief at the Spot Light beer parlor and restaurant found absolutely no evidence of any gambling. At Conners' Lunch near the courthouse the only evidence of possible horseracing bets was a racing form spotted near the phone booth. When the manager was asked if he would take a bet, he said, "Well, we don't make a practice of it." The general feeling in Princeton was that with seven cops checking on the seven taverns, gamblers would rather take their wagers to LaSalle where Tom Cawley would be happy to take their bets.

In early July, Bernard Loparty was ready to make a delivery of a load of punchboards and lucky jars to Andrew Yesinowski, owner of Andy's Tavern at 323 E. Walnut in Oglesby. The 1,200 punchboards came with a note that said $1.50 went to the deliveryman and the manufacturer. The syndicate took $3 per board. The proprietor would still make $48 even after the "winnings" were deducted. Punchboards were a very lucrative sideline in taverns and considered "sucker bets" for those who chose to try their luck winning 50 cents or a very rare $1, $2, or $3 punch. Loparty was caught by the police before he could make his delivery.

LaSalle found itself in the national spotlight when the latest issue of Collier's Magazine hit the stands on July 21. A colored photograph was readily identified by local readers as Duffy's United Cigar Store. The magazine photo showed a female playing a slot machine and was captioned, "Keep the Change Lady." An editorial accompanying the photo indicated that Collier's objected to such a scene. One of their writers had secretly taken the photo months earlier when he was on an uncover assignment exposing the gambling in LaSalle. Gordon

Schendel, the writer, had penned other articles on April 15 and April 22 for a series titled "Illinois Shakedown."

While Peru didn't have quite the reputation of LaSalle, it had its share of gambling in 25 of the city's 30 taverns. Some of these places included Becker and Currie's pool hall and Becker's Tavern on Fourth St., Woodshank's bar on Peoria St., and Yanka's and Sajnaj's taverns on Fifth St. Rather than offering a wall of slot machines, these and other taverns had lucky jars, punch boards, baseball tickets, and card games. According to and open letter to the Peru mayor, Frank Konetshny, the News-Tribune said, "Law enforcement in Peru is a joke, much as it is in LaSalle." The paper advised the mayor to clean up his town before the state police did it for him.

The front-page letter had little impact on the mayor and the police chief, Fred Mathieu, who spent part of the next evening at a band concert at the Star Theater, only a block from the Becker and Currie casino.

The News-Tribune also went on the attack against prostitution in LaSalle County. They reported the "employment" of eight or nine girls at the 199 Club located east of the city limits. The "club" had just reopened after being closed for a year and a half. The paper even gave the sheriff specific directions on the brothel's exact location. "You'll find it on the east side of the road leading to Rockwell, just north of the old limestone quarry. Any taxi driver will show you the way."

The flagrant failure to enforce the laws did have an impact. The Peru mayor finally ordered the police chief to inspect the taverns. After a warning or two, the taverns grudgingly hid their punchboards until the heat was off.

Taverns in Oglesby also came under closer scrutiny. On Oct 7, Chief Herbert Gondolfi arrested Yesinowski, when he refused to close down his gambling operations. Francis "Barney" Shields and Frank Rigazio, owners of the Rigazio and Shields tavern at the four corners in Oglesby, had the same experience. Yesinowski was stubborn and warned the police if they arrested him again, it was the police, who would be in trouble next time.

Punchboards were also confiscated by Illinois state police in Wyanet. A load of over 8½ tons of punchboards, which was being delivered by D.M. Leifer from Chicago, was seized on Sept. 12. The court ordered their destruction. On Oct. 18, the Bureau County highway department took five truckloads from the jail to the city dump, where the boards were burned. The fire lasted several days.

Tom Cawley had a gambling setback in early October when Western Union cut his ticker tape communication, effectively closing down the horse-race book. That was followed by the disconnection of Cawley's 24 telephones by Bell Telephone. He was left with only two public phones for legitimate or emergency needs. The actions were the result of complaints filed by the News-Tribune.

Those problems were overshadowed by events in Chicago. Tom Cawley was called to testify before the Kefauver commission, which was investigating the extent of organized crime in the United States.

Sen. Estes Kefauver used the investigations as a springboard for his political ambitions, twice seeking the nomination for the presidency.

The commission had been to every major city questioning "alleged" members of the syndicate. Finally, they required an appearance of Cawley, who testified in October. Sen. Kefauver found the gambling czar to be a witness who honestly acknowledged gambling in LaSalle. Cawley told the commission he didn't pay protection money to anyone, and 90 percent of the people of LaSalle liked the wide open atmosphere. He also said he owned 62 percent of the LaSalle and Streator gambling places. He was very adamant about the role of the mob. "If the syndicate ever moves in, I'm going to get out."

On Dec. 20, Cawley was again called to testify before the investigating committee. The commission's chief counsel, George Robinson, asked if Cawley's bookmaking and crap games were still operating. Cawley answered, "That is correct." He went on to admit that his business income came from baseball tickets, lucky jars, slot machines, and a little from roulette. Even when he was shut down, the bookmaking continued to operate. He played both sides of the fence politically giving an equal amount ($100) to the Democrats and Republicans.

Cawley candidly answered questions put to him by Senator Kefauver during the Chicago hearings on organized crime in 1950. News-Tribune photo.

Tom Cawley's testimony provided some insight to the extent of Cawley's gambling operations but did not bring it to an end. The battle to close down all gambling would continue for several years. Christmas was approaching, and people turned their attention to shopping and making plans to celebrate the end of 1950. The El Reno was one of many clubs ready to greet the New Year.

1951
WAR RAGES ON IN KOREA

The opening days of the New Year looked ominous as the Chinese Communists continued their military advances to within twelve miles of Seoul. Congress was demanding that the president mobilize the home front. In response to the draft in LaSalle County, 19 men left for induction while 41 men were sent to Chicago for pre-induction physicals. On Jan. 24, a group of 18 men from Marshall County was inducted into the Army. This was the largest group sent from the county since the Korean War began. The draft call was smaller in Putnam County. On Jan. 31, seven men boarded the bus for the trip to the Chicago induction center: Teddy Boggio (Hennepin), Lloyd Larson (formerly of Hennepin), Richard Doyle (Standard), Joe Botoletto (Mark), Everett Rieck, Howard Schrowang, and Lawrence Kunkel (Granville).

Meanwhile on Jan. 18 in Korea, a platoon from the 3rd Armored Recon Co. of the 3rd Div. was entering Kumyangjang-ni when they were ambushed. Initial reports said Cpl. Louis Mutta from Sparland was wounded and taken prisoner by the North Koreans. The government officially listed him as MIA.

Pfc. Bert Cinkovich from Marshall County, was killed in the fighting at Hoengsong, South Korea on Feb. 13. He was in the 38th Inf. Reg. of the 2nd Inf. Div. In that same unit, Pvt. Harry Myers of Mendota was killed the following day fighting in the same area.

Later in the month, the North Koreans and Chinese forced their way back to the 38th parallel. Operation Killer began on Feb. 22. The battle for Hill 166 raged south of Hoengsong east of Seoul. The Americans and Communists engaged in an artillery duel across the Han River.

Lee County lost two men from Dixon in 1951. First Lt. Charles Muhleback was killed in January, and Pfc. George Dempsey was killed at the Punchbowl in North Korea on June 14, while fighting in Operation Piledriver with the 1st Marines.

A marine from Oglesby, F/Sgt. Ed Fristock, was killed June 7 at Waryong-ni. He was awarded the Navy Cross.

As casualties continued to mount, the draft soon included medical professionals under the age of 50. In December, doctors, dentists, and veterinarians were instructed to register at the Selective Service Headquarters at 606½ Court St. in Ottawa. Fifty-nine doctors registered on Jan. 16. Between the two draft boards covering LaSalle County, there were 39 doctors, 19 dentists, and 1 veterinarian.

Doctor Ray Guisti, a doctor from Mark, (right), had been in Korea since early July, 1950. On Feb. 10, 1951, the News-Tribune and the Chicago Tribune described his performance of a "surgical miracle" on a rifleman, who was wounded in the neck and chest. The soldier was brought into the surgical tent, where Guisti was caring for the wounded all night. With blood  filling the young man's lungs and without using anesthetic, Dr. Guisti immediately "opened the soldier's neck, slit the wind pipe, and inserted an air tube." He then began to draw the blood out of the soldier's lungs. Speaking to a Chicago Tribune reporter, Dr. Guisti said, "That was one of the miracles of medicine. It was almost as if the Lord directed my scalpel. My six years of study and internship paid off right there in five minutes. Without the benefit of my two years at the (Cook) County hospital I never could have done it." Dr. Guisti was later awarded the Bronze Star for saving the man's life.

The Mark doctor was featured again on the front page of the News-Tribune on Feb. 24. This time, he was pictured treating a Chinese soldier, who was captured near Seoul.

Other soldiers were also noted for their bravery under fire. Mrs. Marie Collins of Oglesby learned in January that her son, Sgt. Robert R. Honn, was awarded a Bronze Star, the fourth highest decoration for heroism. The incident occurred on

Nov. 5, 1950 near Paekchon. Korea. When his 1st Cavalry artillery unit came under attack by mortars and automatic weapons, Honn moved to an exposed position to direct fire against the enemy. The citation read, "By his selfless courage and skillful leadership in the face of enemy fire, Sgt. Honn contributed materially in repelling the enemy attack."

One of the biggest aerial battles took place on Jan. 23. The 30-minute duel involved 33 F-84s engaging as many as 28 MiGs from a base in Antung, Manchuria. Thunderjet pilots downed four of the MiG-15s and damaged four others.

F-84 Thunderjet (USAF photo)

Russian mechanics prepare a MiG-15 at Antung, Manchuria.

The fighting was brutal in North Korea. Roy C. Johnson had been wounded in the fighting at Kunu-ri and was taken prisoner in December 1950. It was later determined he died of his wounds on Mar. 11, 1951. During the communist advance on Seoul, S/Sgt. John F. Malone of Ottawa was wounded in both knees.

The war was having an effect on the home front. Inflation forced the freezing of wages and prices effective Jan. 25, The six-man Wage Stabilization Board was created by Congress to enforce regulations. Shortages of vital materials resulted in the creation of the National Production Authority. Whitman W. Hopton, assistant to the president of Matthiessen-Hegeler Zinc in LaSalle, was named the new director of the lead and zinc division. His job would be to oversee the conservation of tin, lead, and zinc for the defense industry.

Civilian involvement during the war took in a broader picture of the communist threat. Civil defense for local communities was organized in a variety of ways. The administration of the Ryburn-King Hospital in Ottawa was asked to increase its patient capacity by 76% in case of enemy attack. The hospital board asked Mayor Leamy to call for civilian volunteers for the defense of Ottawa.

Speaking to a group of officials from Spring Valley, Streator, and the Tri-Cities at the LaSalle City Hall on Feb. 2, Maj. Gen. John Homer, assistant to the director of civil defense for Illinois, identified the LaSalle-Peru-Oglesby region as "a critical target area" because of its many industries. Although the general downplayed the possibility of aerial bombardment, including an atomic bomb being dropped on the area, he did not rule out the possibility of industrial sabotage "to cripple or paralyze defense production." The general suggested the adoption of a civil defense plan drawn up for Carlinville, IL. He also discussed the air raid warning signals.

The call for civilian participation was taken to heart by the Granville unit of the Ground Observation Corps (GOC) as they participated in a nationwide practice alert on Feb. 10-11. Volunteer airplane spotters manned their post at Hopkins H.S. on a two-hour rotating schedule from 8 a.m. until 4 p.m.

The Granville GOC volunteers watched for Russian bombers from their vantage point on top of the Hopkins H.S.

Participants included Francis Ballerine, E. R. Harris, J. A. Wallace, Vernon Lamb, Chester Novak, Sam Kaletka, William Glover, Dr. R. M. Germano, Robert Kidd, Pete Pesante, and Leo Utterback. The female volunteers included Mrs. Quentin Tyler, Mrs. Francis Ballerine, Mrs. G. H. Sandberg, Mrs. Brunis Captani, Mrs. Glenn Holmbeck, Mrs. Alvin Peterson, Mrs. Frank Serrine Jr., Mrs. Clarence Trovero, Mrs. John Buhn, and Mrs. Lyle Young. Julius Hansen was the supervisor of the area GOC. Charles Kassabaum headed the local GOC with assistants, Laurence Ellena, and August Nelson. Volunteers received a lapel badge to indicate their membership in the corps. During a two-day test, Kassabaum reported sightings of 49 planes to the Chicago filter center.

Fritz Ballerine, one of the GOC volunteers, recalled that exercise. In WWII, he worked on B-17s at Maxwell Airfield in Alabama and was also trained in the identification of aircraft. As a member of the Granville civil defense unit during the 1951 drill, he said the group took turns watching for unknown planes from their vantage point on the roof of Hopkins H. S. Pairs of airplane spotters scanned the skies looking for "enemy" planes. One plane in particular caught their attention because it had no identification numbers painted on the fuselage or wings. However, they were not worried because it was a biplane, most likely a crop duster. Nonetheless, the incident was reported to the Chicago center.

Wenona's GOC was also active during the alert. Oral Axline and George Braymen erected a small shelter on the roof of the Goodwin Garage. An oil stove was installed to fight off the chilly February weather. Nine aircraft were reported by the observers, who were presented with silver lapel pins from the Eastern Air Defense Command in appreciation for their work.

Some civilians were looking for something besides Russian bombers flying over the country. Ever since the July 8, 1947 report that a flying disk had crashed near Roswell, N.M., there had been additional sightings of flying saucers.

Certain events heightened those fears. The 1950 release of "The Flying Saucer" in local movie theaters drew more attention to the phenomenon. About the same time, Look Magazine published a story by a naval officer explaining the reason behind so many sightings. According to the Navy version, the sightings were actually Skyhook balloons (right), launched to measure cosmic rays at high altitudes. The 100-foot 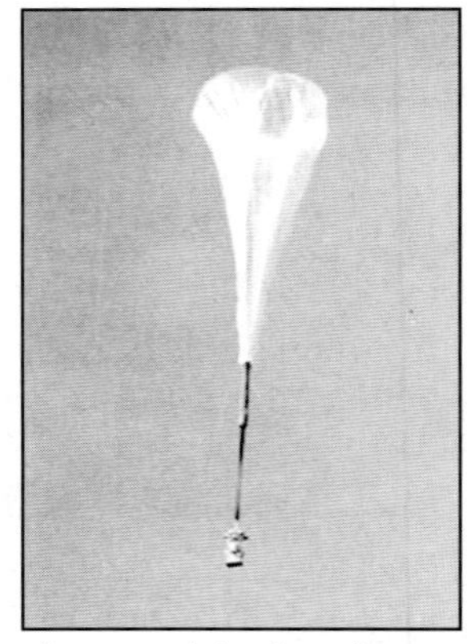 diameter balloons appeared saucer-shaped at an altitude of over 70,000 feet. The jet stream moved them across the sky at 200 mph. The number of balloon launchings, which began in 1947, seemed to match the number of flying saucer sightings over Midwestern states.

Disaster preparedness was still a key issue whether it concerned aliens from outer space or bombers from the Soviet

Union. When officers of the Tri-City Red Cross chapter met at the Hotel Kaskaskia on Feb. 21, Ed Weerts of Peru, the chapter's disaster relief chairman, reported that 90% of the work in preparedness had been achieved.

THAT'S ENTERTAINMENT

Most Illinois Valley residents were more likely to take a greater interest in having a good time rather than constantly worrying about nuclear war. Casinos, like Kelly and Cawley's, brought in a variety of performers for weekend shows.

Many musical groups had been featured on national television, and local residents could finally see them in person. "The Dozier Boys," a black quintet, appeared for three nights in late February at the El Reno cocktail club located two miles west of Ottawa on Rt. 6. Tinney Cosgrove hired "Jump" Jackson & His Red-Hot Band to perform in March at the Silver Congo. Along with Jackson, patrons would enjoy songstress Helen Russel.

William "Tinney" Cosgrove Jr. Photo contributed by Anna Lijewski.

On Feb. 12, Horace Heidt appeared in Ottawa with his "Stars on Parade" variety show. One of the acts was the Bud Messenie Quartet. Gordon Powers and Larry Marta attended the L-P-O Junior College. Heidt thought the quartet was very good, and they were considered to participate on Heidt's "Original Youth Opportunity Program," which began as a radio broadcast in 1947 and continued as a television series.

In this News-Tribune photo of Heidt are Bud Messenie from Ottawa, Gordon Powers from Peru, and Paul Brinkman and Larry Marta from Ottawa.

Buzz Verucchi was a showman who brought some of the biggest names in musical entertainment to Spring Valley. His establishment was also used for a roller-skating rink most evenings.

This ad in the Mar. 7, 1951 edition of the News-Tribune illustrates one of the groups that performed in Spring Valley.

Movies were a big draw on the weekends, and Hollywood churned out many westerns, war films, mysteries, and comedies. In DePue, Dennis Morgan was staring in "God is My Co-Pilot" at the Palace. The management of the Majestic in LaSalle apologized to its patrons because there would only be one matinee performance of Gary Cooper and Ruth Roman in "Dallas" due to the need to install plush seating in the mezzanine.

E. E. Alger, the entrepreneur, who gained a reputation for theater management during the Depression, celebrated his 40th anniversary in the business in 1951. One of his improvements in Peru was the renovation of the old Star movie theater, which was refurbished and renamed the Art Theater. He scheduled the grand opening of his Art Theater on Easter Sunday, Mar. 25. He gave Hawaiian orchids to the first 200 ladies, who came to see "The Red Shoes."

On that same date in Spring Valley, Tommy Reed and his orchestra were playing at a Les-Buzz dance. The $1.25 admission was being donated to the Dominic Oberto American Legion's building fund.

Buzz Verucchi used flyers and this car to advertise coming events.

Colorful postcards were distributed to draw the crowds to the Les-Buzz skating rink and dance hall. Dick Verucchi collection.

In recognition of the men stationed overseas, the News-Tribune lowered its annual subscription rate to $9.00 to send the paper to anyone in the armed forces. Readers were kept informed of soldiers such as Cpl. Donald Baznik of LaSalle, a WWII veteran, who was called back to fight in Korea, where he was wounded. Staff Sgt. Sam Storage, another LaSalle resident, was photographed performing his duties as an armorer for F-80 Shooting Stars while assigned to the 49th Fighter Bomber Wing of the 5th Air Force.

The war on communism was also being waged in America. After over seven hours of deliberations, a jury returned a guilty verdict against Julius and Ethel Rosenberg on Mar. 29 for delivering classified documents about the atomic bomb to the Soviets. They were sentenced to die in the electric chair. In spite of numerous appeals to the US Supreme Court and requests for a presidential pardon, they were executed for espionage on June 19, 1953.

Co-conspirators Morton Sobell and David Greenglass, the brother of Ethel, were also found guilty of spying. They received long prison sentences.

Gen. MacArthur's conduct of the war was a source of frustration to President Truman. The general's advocacy of involving of Chinese Nationalists on Formosa to open a second front and the encouragement of bombing Red China were in direct conflict with Truman's goal of a limited war. Finally, Truman fired MacArthur and replaced him with Gen. Matthew Ridgeway. It was an unpopular move in the eyes of many Americans, who held MacArthur in high regard. On April 18, the LaSalle Board of Supervisors passed a resolution expressing the appreciation of the people of LaSalle for MacArthur's "loyalty, devotion, and service in their cause."

A crowd, estimated at 7.5 million, greeted Gen. MacArthur when he arrived in New York City. On April 26, the general flew in his private plane, *Bataan*, to Midway airport in Chicago, where he was welcomed with a 17-gun salute by 5th Army artillerymen. A motorcade drove down 55th Street to a

Chicago hotel. In the evening, a recognition celebration was held at Soldier's Field.

Among those on hand to welcome the general was the American Legion drum and bugle unit from Ottawa Post 33. After marching in the colorful parade before the general's arrival at the stadium, the Ottawa men took their seats at the west end of Soldiers Field, where they had a good view of MacArthur when his car circled the stadium.

After the ceremonies in Chicago, the general's motorcade proceeded to Milwaukee, making short stops in Evanston, Winnetka, Highland Park, Ft. Sheridan, and Great Lakes. The entourage continued through Waukegan, Kenosha, and Racine before finally arriving in Milwaukee. MacArthur then returned to Chicago and flew back to New York City. He continued to make numerous speeches defending his motives and actions in disagreement with the president.

In the meantime, the fighting near Seoul grew more intense. The Chinese gained ground on the western front following the Yonchon-Uijonbu invasion route.

On June 2, there was heartbreaking news for Mrs. Lourine Armstrong. Her son, Cpl. Bryan Armstrong, a Wenona H.S. graduate, was killed at Chaun-ni in Korea on May 17. He was the first soldier from Wenona to lose his life in the war.

LeRoy Lauf received word that his brother, Pfc. John W. Lauf, a 20-year old Wenona native and paratrooper serving with the 187th Airborne, was wounded at Wonton-ni and died of his wounds on June 14, 1951.

About that same time, Pfc. Robert Schaibley from Tonica was home on medical leave to visit his parents in Leonore. He was awarded the Purple Heart with cluster having been wounded a second time while fighting in Korea. After his 30-day furlough, he reported to the hospital in Battle Creek, MI.

Another solider who was a recipient of a Purple Heart was Pfc. Edward Marliere of DePue, who was wounded on June 10.

Capt. Robert Klein of the 182nd Fighter Bomber Squadron was flying his F-84E near Wonsan, North Korea when a shell from enemy anti-aircraft fire hit his plane on July 25. He was listed as a MIA but presumed dead at the end of the year. His sister Lucille Klein later honored him at a memorial ceremony in Streator. Photo from the Korean War Project.

Souvenir postcard of the USNS *Marine Lynx*. US Navy photo.

Some of the men were finally returning to the Illinois Valley. The *Marine Lynx*, a navy transport carrying 2,439 soldiers was due in the port of Seattle on July 6. Aboard the ship were 91 men from Illinois including Pfc. Donald Siekierka from Peru, Roy J. Neuhalfen of Seatonville, and Pfc. Tom Sroka of Ottawa. The ship was the tenth one returning as part of the army's rotation program.

THE BEEF WAR

Families on the home front during the war faced rising food prices and shortages. Cattlemen were enraged by the mandatory prices for livestock being sent to the stockyards. Michael DiSalle, the government price czar, had the unenviable job of enforcing a 10¢ per pound rollback on live cattle sales effective May 10. Some of the packers like Armour and Co. at the Chicago stockyards complained that the restrictions had forced a virtual shutdown of their operations since cattlemen refused to ship cattle at government-controlled prices. The shortages were soon apparent in local supermarkets, where meat sales were generally restricted to pork and chicken. Beef was available but at inflated prices. DiSalle argued that the restrictions were necessary to prevent the type of black marketing the Office of Price Administration faced in WWII. More government-imposed price reductions were scheduled for August and October with the goal of reducing prices for consumers.

This ad from the June 28, 1951 edition of the News-Tribune announced the grand opening of the LaSalle Supermarket at 163 Marquette. One unusual aspect of the ad is the apparent availability of beef products. By comparison other grocers' ads featured pork and chicken, but few beef cuts.

Newspaper coverage of the fighting in Korea in June focused more on aerial dogfights over the 38th parallel. Ground fighting was stalemated with attacks and counter-attacks. By July, the Reds seemed to be willing to sit down at an armistice meeting with Ridgeway at Kaesong to end the 53-week war. However, the fighting continued as the UN forces captured a 3,500-foot mountain peak south of Pyongyang in a 3-day pitched battle with 5,000 Chinese defenders.

SURRENDER IN THE GAMBLING WAR?

The Chinese may have been driven from their hilltop position, but the LaSalle gambling establishments were still fighting to stay in business. Addressing a city council meeting on Mar. 6, LaSalle mayor Bildhauer said, "I am here and now giving the chief orders to put down gambling. There is more gambling going on in LaSalle now than when the Kefauver committee looked into it." But, would lasting action be taken?

Two days later, nothing had changed. Sheriff Harbeck promised that all gambling would be down by the end of the week. The tavern operators finally complied, and the slot machines were out of sight as of midnight on Saturday, However, the Silver Congo still had its crap table, and Tom Cawley's casino was still running a lottery on Sunday. Gambling countywide was down with those exceptions. A raid at Kelly and Cawley's and Johnny Essl's by Harbeck's men on April 8 did result in the confiscation of money boards at both locations and some dice and chips at Cawley's.

LaSalle police chief Kasprowicz complained that when he personally made inspections, everything disappeared, and as soon as he left, gambling resumed. During his inspection of over 80 taverns, he only found gambling at the Rocket Bar across from the Rock Island Depot. Ray Sroberts was playing the lucky jar tickets. The chief arrested the patron and ordered Frank Zupancic Jr., the owner, to appear before the court on the charge of operating a lottery. There was no action at Cawley's; the gambling room at the Silver Congo had become a dining room; and the spinner had been moved away from the bar at the Rose Bowl.

As soon as the sheriff left for a downstate convention on April 20, the casinos were back in business. Cawley had a crap table, poker, punchboards, and lucky jars. Black Jack and poker games were active at Cosgrove's Silver Congo. The Rose Bowl had a poker game. However, the smaller places, including the Senate, El Mirador, and the Maples, were clean. When the sheriff returned, Cawley closed his upstairs casino operations in LaSalle and Streator.

The crackdown in LaSalle didn't stop gambling in Ottawa. However, most of the action was limited to ticket boards and lucky jars at the Senate, Lena's Tap, and The Steakhouse. The bookie at the D. and W. east of the courthouse was still taking bets on horse races.

The raids produced sparse results in the following weeks. On Thursday, April 26, a poker game at Cawley's was broken up. The five players were all unemployed casino workers. About 90 workers were laid off at the Paddock and Cawley's casino during the crackdown. The case was dismissed on April 27; the officers never had a search warrant.

Sheriff W. C. Duffield in Bureau County also made an effort to stop gambling. He visited Harry Cassiday, owner of Cassidy's Spring Valley casino, and told him to close down like the other places of gambling. Cassidy complied; the lucky jars simply disappeared under the counters.

Periodically, there were also vice raids on "Bawdy House Row," located east of LaSalle in Rockwell. On May 21, "Lucky" Hedgepath was charged with disorderly conduct and paid a $200 fine. "Jackie" Martin was fined $100 on the same charge. About a month later, Marie, the madam at the Gay Mill brothel, and Ruby and Joann, two of her employees, lost several hundred dollars at the Rose Bowl's blackjack table and raised hell. The police were called, but the women would not give their names nor sign a complaint.

Women enjoyed their gambling, and Kelly and Cawley's was well-known for its second floor bingo games and three-player crap games.

Bingo tumbler used at Cawley's. ▶

OTHER DIVERSIONS

While the fighting in Korea and the gambling raids captured most of the front-page news, there were other stories of interest in the Illinois Valley. An old Liberty ship, converted into an ore carrier was making its 2,000-mile journey from Baltimore to Lake Michigan by way of the Illinois River. What made the news so intriguing was the size of the *Cliffs Victory*. It was cut in half, and a 165-foot section was added, making the ship 620-feet long. The locks on the river were only designed for ships 600-feet long. In addition, the bridges in some sections of the river only had a clearance of 46'5", but the ship measured 53'8" from keel to the top of the bridge. To pass through the locks, it was necessary to empty all ballast and weld air-tight pontoons to the hull to lift the ship's bow and stern over the gates. Not many residents were up at 2 a.m. on May 5 to see the transit of the ship at the Starved Rock locks.

After passing through the Marseilles, Brandon Road, and Lockport locks, the captain of the *Cliffs Victory* faced the problem of navigating under numerous bridges, especially the Van Buren St. Bridge in Chicago. The only way to safely pass under the bridges was by taking on as much ballast as possible clearing the river bottom by as little as one foot. It arrived in Chicago on May 9.

It was a spectacle to watch large ships moving through the locks. Only a few days after the passage of the *Cliffs Victory*, another large ship, the 400-foot *Daniel Pierce*, an oil tanker, was pushed by a tug through the locks. Another ore boat, the 600-foot *Tom Girdler*, passed through the locks on Sept. 22. A sizeable crowd was on hand to watch the ship moving through the locks at Starved Rock that evening.

A larger ship, the *Marine Angel* (a.k.a. *McKee Sons*), measuring 633 feet long, passed through the Marseilles locks on Mar. 5, 1953. Digital image collection from Fr. Edward J. Dowling, S. J., Marine Historical Collection, University of Detroit Mercy.

Others were more interested in watching television. Small black and white sets had been very popular when they first came on the market after WWII. The consoles were fitted with picture tubes measuring from 10-inches to the latest 1951 sets with 17-inch screens.

Most people had to settle for black and white TV's. A 17" screen was considered to be a quality set in 1951. Reprinted from May 4, 1951 edition of News-Tribune.

CBS and RCA were experimenting with two versions of color TV's. The dispute over a standardized system ended in an 8-0 Supreme Court decision stating the FCC had the right to pick one system as the national standard. That was the CBS color spinning wheel version. RCA's argument that its three-color tube was cheaper than the CBS system, which required a spinning wheel in front of a black/white TV to view pictures in color, was rejected. That decision was reversed on Dec. 17, 1953, and the RCA system was adopted. The first color program was broadcast on Oct. 20, 1951.

Just as Ottawa had its moment in the movie limelight in 1950 with the "Rock Island Trail" production, LaSalle also had a bit of the Hollywood spotlight with the arrival of western star Rex Allen at the LaSalle Theater. Allen's appearance at the LaSalle Theater was used to promote his latest film, "Rodeo King and the Senorita." Allen appeared on stage for three of the shows and sang western songs while playing his guitar. He also drew out his silver-handled six-shooters and fired them.

This publicity photo was used in the News-Tribune to advertise the appearance of Rex Allen at the LaSalle Theater on July 26.

After the Greater LaSalle County Association handed out 2,000 Rex Allen publicity photos, a large crowd sought Allen's autograph. Festivities for the 14th annual LaSalle County Day continued on Friday, when 18,340 persons came to Starved Rock State Park. Activities included children's foot races, and performances by unicycle artists, acrobats, and a balancing team.

NAILING DOWN THE LID ON VICE

Occasionally, LaSalle sheriff's deputies raided the local brothels. On July 10, they paid a visit to the Club 199 south of Rt. 6, a mile east of LaSalle, and the Elms, which was located near the courthouse in Ottawa. Two days later, another raid was conducted at Gay Mill in Jonesville, where they arrested the madam, Jean Collinski, and Helen Meyer, one of the "inmates," as the press referred to prostitutes. The charge of running a "disorderly house" brought with it a fine of $200. The judge only fined the "inmate" $100.

It must have been a quite a surprise to read in the News-Tribune on Friday, July 13, the building used as the sleeping quarters for the girls of Club 199 was burned to the ground during the night. Fortunately, the place was unoccupied after the raid. The mysterious fire leveled the building, which was last known to be operated by "Lucky" Hedgepath. However, he had not operated the place since Sheriff Harbeck conducted a raid there in May.

The fire was reported by a cab driver at 2:20 a.m., but by the time the Utica fire department arrived, the house was burned down to the foundation. The firemen managed to keep the fire from spreading to Club 199.

Closing down "bawdy house lane" and other areas of prostitution was not a top priority for the local police departments. With the major casinos in the cities operating on a limited basis, the state police decided to raid ten rural taverns on Route 23 between Ottawa and Streator. These included Club Grove, the Gables, the Farm, El Camino Lounge, Stoney's, Otto's Tavern, Club Del Monte, Blatz Tavern, Club Indian Acres, and the Schlitz Tavern. The July 20 raid resulted in the seizure of 29 slot machines and $1,590 in coins.

The raids continued in early September in the Tri-Cities. Lucky jars and punchboards were seized at several First Street businesses including the Clover Club, the Hub, and Club Devon. In Oglesby the police raided the Diamond Horseshoe and the K& S Tap. The only spot in Peru found with illegal paraphernalia was Becker and Currie on Fourth St. Two places in Spring Valley were in violation of the law, Baracani's and Pohl's Tavern.

Acting on complaints about continued gambling at the end of September, Bureau County sheriff Duffield's men raided the Vitaphone Tavern on Rt. 29 near DePue and the Hill Top Tavern in Buda. Other investigations in Neponset and Mineral failed to result in any criminal charges.

Less than a week after these raids, the police found lucky jars and punch boards at the Globe Tavern, The Hub Tavern, Trahd's Tavern, and the Big House in Spring Valley. Those accused generally paid a $125 fine and court costs. Louis Bonucci had to pay $250; this was his second offense.

The state police continued their sweep through the area confiscating 23 one-armed bandits found in the following locations: Hoghouse (Somonauk), Sportsman's Inn (Sheridan), Century House (Earlville), and three locations in Mendota, the Red Rose Tavern, the Conoco truck stop and tavern, and the Bowlair Cocktail Lounge. The judge fined each owner $100 and ordered the destruction of the machines.

Pictured is one of the 25¢ slot machines used at the Kelly and Cawley casino. It is now part of Tom Cawley II's collection of gambling memorabilia. Photo by author.

Even with the extensive raids, gambling continued. In December, a new federal law required the purchase of a tax stamp to accept wagers at a location other than where the even took place. LaSalle County initially led the state with 284 applications. Tom Cawley and his family applied for 30 of the stamps, which cost $33.34 each. Dozens of restaurants, taverns and casinos from Lostant to Ottawa dominated the downstate requests. The News-Tribune dubbed LaSalle the "Gambling Center of the United States." Cook County only had 54 applications, and Marshall County had the third highest number of applications. The LaSalle paper published the names and address of all of the applicants making it very easy for the local state's attorneys and police officials to conduct raids.

It didn't take long to put together a hit list. A few days after the list of stamp purchasers was published, the Streator police raided nine of the 100 locations that applied for stamps. Raids were conducted at four cigar stores: Rarton's, Volkman's, Miller's, and Proud's; and four taverns: Pratt Brothers, Hunter's, Pano's, and Savage's.

Proud's Cigar Store at 222 E. Main St., was one of the places raided in Streator. Streator Historical Society photo.

The Paddock Club was also on the list since it was well-known for gambling on the second floor. The police only confiscated one slot machine at each location as evidence.

Even though the registration for tax stamps confirmed the probable location of gambling, it was not a guarantee of any violation of the law according to Mayor Bildhauer. Apparently, the local businesses didn't want to violate federal law. Three more operators purchased the stamps: Ficek's Lounge and the Come Back Inn on First Street in LaSalle and Shine's Hillbilly Club in Jonesville. By the end of the year, LaSalle County topped the list with 358 stamps issued. Peoria County was a distant second with 174. Cook County purchasers ranked sixth with only 101 stamps.

The effort to stamp out gambling progressed about as slowly as the Korean peace talks in the fall of 1951. The North Koreans and the Americans each claimed that the other side had bombed the Kaesong neutral area.

Occasionally, friends and relatives of local servicemen would learn about the status of the men overseas. Perry B. Bartram of Tonica, one of the area's WWII veterans, who survived the Japanese attack at Hickam Field on Dec. 7, 1941, was in Korea as platoon sergeant in the 629th Medical Clearing Company in central Korea. As a result of action in the Battle of Soyang, he was promoted to Master Sergeant on July 1.

Cpl. Jack Marynus was one of the soldiers from LaSalle, who was badly wounded on Sept. 17 in the fighting north of Yangu on Bloody Ridge, where fighting had raged on for 18 days. Marynus was taken to an aid station, where he received six pints of blood. He was then flown to Osaka, Japan where he needed an operation and another 14 units of blood. His experience made him realize how important blood donations were for the hundreds of other wounded soldiers in Korea. The L-P graduate promised that he would become a donor to repay those who donated the blood that saved his life.

Another soldier highlighted in the local news was Sgt. Eugene R. Brown from Peru. He was in charge of the No. 1 gun of Battery A of the 82nd Field Artillery when they fired the battalion's 200,000 round. In the intense fighting around Yonchon, the battalion fired a record-breaking 5,816 rounds in one day.

Pfc. William Bacidore of LaSalle, another former L-P student, had a very different assignment. While a member of the 17th Infantry Regiment, he was assigned to guard the UN truce negotiator camp at Munson near Panmunjom. It was an improvement over his unit's recent battles on Bloody Ridge.

The hill battles along the 38th parallel continued through July and September. Marine Pfc. Richard A. Brooks from Toluca was killed in the fighting at the Punchbowl on Sept. 12.

In the days that followed, the LaSalle newspaper described the biggest air battles of the war pitting MiG-15s against F-86 Sabre jets. In one day in late September, 254 jets from both sides were involved. In the morning, 75 UN planes took on 120 MiGs and downed or damaged 14 enemy jets. Again outnumbered in the afternoon, 24 Thunderjets engaged 35 MiGs. Meanwhile, little was being accomplished by the truce negotiators, who were meeting at Panmunjom, Korea.

In late November 1951, the USAF intercepted one of the biggest formations of Chinese and North Korean aircraft seen in MiG Alley. A flight of 30 Tu-2 bombers and 16 La-9 fighter-bombers crossed the Yalu River. This was the first mass formation of enemy bombers seen in the fighting. They were engaged by a flight of 31 American F-86 Sabre jets. One La-9 and nine of the enemy bombers were shot down.

Above is a Russian Tu-2. Although the Reds mainly flew MiG-15's in the Korean War, they also had some La-9's, a post-WWII Russian fighter. Below: This is the last remaining airworthy La-9.

UTICA CELEBRATES ITS HISTORY

Headline stories switched from Korea to events in Utica in October. The village became the focal point for the re-enactment of the arrival of a Jesuit missionary, Father Marquette, in 1675. On Oct. 14, 1951, a granite and marble memorial was dedicated as part of the event.

Thousands of people came to Utica to watch the re-enactment of the arrival of Father Pere Marquette, Louis Joliet, Jacques LeCastor, and Pierre Porteret.
Utica library photo.

The Illinois Valley Council of the Knights of Columbus planned a number of ceremonies. Father Martin Coughlin, pastor of St. Mary's Church in Utica, conducted the research concerning Marquette's celebration of the first Easter Mass in Illinois and the founding of the mission at Utica. The re-enactors, all from Ottawa, were Gerald Rondeau (Father Marquette), Bernard Sexton, (Joliet), Thomas Benson (voyager), and Richard Miller (voyager). Participants also included 23 members of the Menominee Indians from northern Wisconsin, who greeted the French explorers on the south bank of the Illinois River.

The Indians and French explorers proceeded to an altar erected at Starved Rock campground. The next to arrive were Archbishop Joseph Schlarman of Peoria and Bishop Martin McNamara of Joliet, Others gathering for the religious service included the Knights of Columbus, Catholic War Veterans, Boy Scouts, the 90-member Palestrina choir of Peoria, and a 600-voice choir consisting of Catholic high school students from the Peoria diocese.

Assisting at the service were Msgr. Francis Cleary of St. Columba's Church in Ottawa, Msgr. L. J. Wissing of Mendota, Msgr. F. P. Blecke of Peoria and other priests from LaSalle, Naplate, Ottawa, and Peru. Other dignitaries included Gov. Adlai Stevenson, Senator Everett Dirksen, and Francois Briere, the French consul general of Chicago.

Father Coughlin welcomed the guests. According to Indian tradition, the chalice used at the field mass was the same one used by Father Marquette during his work in Michigan.

Chief Payetanimah presented Archbishop Schlarman with an Indian headdress, making him an honorary member of the Menominee tribe. Utica library photos.

During the ceremonies, Cardinal Samuel Stritch of Chicago unveiled the Marquette memorial. Though the dedication event took place almost 60 years ago, the memorial, which is located on the grounds of the St. Mary's Church in Utica, reminds passersby of the efforts of Father Marquette to bring Christianity to the Indians by establishing the first mission in the Illinois country. Photo by author.

WINTER WEATHER CAUSES HAVOC

The memories of the Utica memorial service soon faded as violent weather patterns spread across the Illinois Valley. On Thursday, Dec. 7, at 6 p.m., a tornado began twisting its way across Spring Valley. The greatest damage occurred in the southeast section of the city, where four of the five houses on South Gallagher St. were destroyed. Seventeen residents, including eleven children, were left homeless. Joseph Savitch, was the lone fatality. His death was caused by the fatal injuries he suffered when the Northwestern railroad depot was blown over by the high winds, and the debris fell on him and another man, Edward Siekierka, who was injured.

After the storm subsided, most of the homeless were given shelter by neighbors. Duane Page and his wife and seven children stayed in St. Margaret's Hospital. Henry Wallaert was found suffering shock and a few bruises but was otherwise unhurt in his basement; the entire second floor was swept away. Lorenzo Calzia sought safety during the storm in the basement of the Barnarto house, where he was residing. The Schmollinger home was also wrecked. An unoccupied fourth house was moved off its foundation. Twisted steel beams from a Western Sand and Gravel building fell on five of their ready-mix cement trucks. Other damage included the garage warehouse of the Valley Builders and the CB&Q depot, which was completely leveled.

Alex J. Blassick served as the station agent of the CB&Q depot in Spring Valley before it was destroyed by the twister. Photo contributed by Helen Thomas.

In the rural areas, the tornado also struck a number of farm buildings. Three structures in the Troy Grove area were damaged. As the storm moved to the northeast, it blew away part of the porch and blew in the windows of the Wylie Anderson farmhouse ten miles northeast of LaSalle. The winds tore off two chimneys, knocked down four trees, and blew in four windows on the Wayne Zimmerlein farm on Route 51.

December was also remembered for the 16.4" snowfall on the Tri-Cities. On Thursday night, Dec. 20, howling winds, gusting to 45 mph, added six inches of new snow across most of northern Illinois. Drifting snow limited travel to one lane south of the Tri-Cities. The Rt. 51 highway was completely blocked south of Wenona. Princeton was totally isolated in all directions. The road between Princeton and Tiskilwa was clogged with over 30 vehicles. Drifting snow blocked Rt. 34 at Earlville. Rt. 6 between Ottawa and LaSalle had some one-way traffic, but there were many stalled cars. No traffic was moving between Ladd and Spring Valley. The snowstorm had paralyzed most of the traffic from Peoria north and west to the Mississippi River. The winds were diminishing, but a new cold front moved through the Illinois Valley. The next day, roads were covered with ten-foot drifts. Rt. 23 north of Ottawa was closed. Travel over Route 71 to Rt. 52 was impossible as was travel on Rt. 34 from Princeton to Mendota and Earlville.

In spite of the terrible weather, the raids on gambling casinos, and the fighting in Korea, there were a few positive reminders of 1951. The news from Korea indicated the Communists might be ready to talk about a truce. Lists of the POW's were exchanged, and there was hope that the 3,198 Americans and over 8,000 other allies on the lists might be exchanged for the 132,472 Communist soldiers held by the UN.

On New Year's Eve, there was one more bit of uplifting news. Cpl. Ollis Popplewell from Utica was awarded a Bronze Star with a "V" device for valor. The medal was awarded in recognition for action in August 1951 when he volunteered to lay phone lines and repair wires that were broken by hostile enemy fire. By connecting the damaged lines, while under heavy machine gun and sniper fire, he insured the communications needed for the success of each mission.

1952
NO ROOM FOR GAMBLING

January began with a transformation in the Kelly-Cawley business. On Monday, Jan. 14, all of the gambling paraphernalia disappeared. Instead of offering tickets from a lucky jar, there was only candy, gum and cigarettes to be purchased. Most of the employees were laid off. One former employee said he was going over to Second Street for a job. He was referring to the Illinois State Employment Office at 736 Second Street. Former customers were going to the United Cigar Store at 541 First St. where they had no trouble purchasing tickets or buying a chance on the punchboards.

Other popular gaming establishments followed Cawley's lead. The lights were out at the Rose Bowl on Monday night. A black cloth covered the crap table at the Silver Congo, where only two bartenders were at work.

On Wednesday at the Ottawa courthouse, Cawley was accused of operating a public nuisance by having a casino operation. Judge William Hibbs denied the defense motion that under common law that was not the case. The witnesses against Cawley testified there was a crap table being used, and a card game in progress. However, they also admitted that they had not received any complaints from those who were gambling or the wives of husbands who had lost money at the tables. The trial adjourned on the following Monday afternoon. Judge Hibbs finally ruled that Cawley could no longer operate his business as a gambling house. He concluded the Illinois courts repeatedly held gambling operations to be a public nuisance and issued an injunction preventing any kind of gambling in Cawley's building.

The big time gambling at Cawley's casinos appeared to be over. However, Cawley's Senate Bar, the El Mirador, and the Rose Bowl were up and running with crap tables, card games, and more. LaSalle bars, such as Stachowiak's at Eighth and Crosat Streets and Clem's Tavern at Eighth and Tonti, still had punchboards and lucky jars. Peru's taverns, including the Singapore and the Green Front on Fifth Street and Al's Tap, the 101 Club, the New Moon Tavern, Dick's Place, and the Friendly Tavern on First Street, all had lucky jars and punchboards.

The El Mirador nightclub was located at the north end of the Hotel Francis in LaSalle.

Photo from Anna (Cosgrove) Lijewski collection.

The Rose Bowl was located on First St. west of the Vendome hotel. Photo by author.

Various types of gambling were still available in Spring Valley. News-Tribune investigators discovered in August that of the 38 taverns and other businesses they visited, 29 had gambling devices, usually lucky jars and punchboards. Following that disclosure, Spring Valley Mayor pro temp Sam Sebastian told the paper that all gambling was out in the city. That statement appeared to be correct in most establishments. However, investigators were still able to buy tickets on a punchboard at Cassiday Brothers Billiards at 129 E. St. Paul Street.

In November, a new state's attorney, Harland Warren, was elected. He promised to enforce the anti-gambling laws and personally met with area mayors to seek the strict enforcement of the law. A News-Tribune reporter asked Mayor Bildhauer for his reaction to the initiative by Warren. The mayor simply said, "All will be informed." Warren's threat of strict enforcement of the anti-gambling law without any exceptions didn't seem to make any difference to the bar and casino owners. Gambling was "unabated in LaSalle, Ottawa, Streator, and the other communities" according to the paper.

When the annual federal stamps had to be purchased, LaSalle County led the way. By Dec. 11, residents purchased 444 stamps. Only 295 stamps were sold in Cook County. By the end of the year, Oglesby, Streator and Ottawa appeared to be complying with Warren's demands. But, in LaSalle and Peru, the clamp-down was more of a cat and mouse game. Hoping the big city mayors would fall into line, Warren ordered a raid at the Sportsmen's Inn near Sheridan, where they found three slot machines. Marten's Tavern in Ottawa was also targeted. There the raiders found two of the one-armed bandits. The fines ranged from $200 to $300. It appeared that gambling was finally coming to an end in LaSalle and Bureau counties.

There were other things besides gambling to enjoy. Buzz Verucchi arranged a special engagement of Louis Armstrong on July 26, 1952. For only $2 patrons could dance from 9 p.m. til 1 a.m. The first 50 girls received one of Armstrong's records.

Louis Armstrong and Buzz Verucchi. Dick Verucchi collection.

HOME FRONT READINESS

There was a more serious side to life in the Illinois Valley. Stories of military personnel were generally limited to reports of servicemen, who were promoted, awarded medals for valor, or missing, wounded, or killed in Korea. One soldier from Oglesby, Pfc. Angelo Nicoli, returned from Korea after having seen firsthand the medical needs of the wounded. While home on emergency leave, Nicoli was photographed by the News-Tribune with Mrs. Charles Korn as he prepared to donate blood at the bloodmobile at the Baptist Church.

THE LAST TO BE CALLED?

As American casualties mounted, and rotation continued in Korea, the government activated certain National Guard units. In February, the 44th Infantry Regiment was called to duty. The regiment included Ottawa's mortar and medical companies, LaSalle's Infantry Company L, Peru's headquarters company, as well as units from other cities.

On Feb. 18, thousands of friends and relatives gave the men of the 44th patriotic sendoffs in Ottawa and LaSalle. In Ottawa, the Elks, VFW, American Legion, Ottawa H.S., drum and bugle corps and boys' drill team marched with the soldiers from the armory to the Rock Island depot. In LaSalle, the L-P band and color guard met the soldiers who assembled at the armory. They marched down to the railroad depot, where the guardsmen boarded the Peoria *Rocket* troop train to join other units in Rock Island. Their next destination was Camp Cooke, CA. There they would train for nine months before being sent to Korea. According to the Army, the 44th might be the last reserve unit called to duty for the Korean War.

MARINES PREPARE FOR NUCLEAR WAR

While many marines were engaged in the hill fighting in Korea, others were training in the Nevada desert to determine the effects of an atomic bomb detonation. Among the 2,000 marines in the test on May 1, 1952 at Camp Desert Rock, NV were five men from the Illinois Valley. Sgt. William Casserly (Oglesby), Sgt. Ralph Hughett (LaSalle), Sgt. Louis A. Strom (LaSalle), Cpl. Ray C. Kotowski (LaSalle), and Pfc.

David G. Losey (LaMoille) were among those who would be in foxholes located only four miles from "ground zero."

At 8:30 a.m., a low-yield atomic bomb (19 kilotons) was dropped from an altitude of 1,040 feet by a B-45 flying over the Nevada Test Site. USAF photo of a B-45.

After the explosion, two battalions of marines got out of their foxholes and advanced to within 500 yards of ground zero.

Gen. Joseph Burger described the results of Operation Snapper on test dummies. Those in foxholes were barely damaged, but those above ground and further away from the blast were completely destroyed. The military equipment was burning or smashed. An M-7 tank was found flipped on its back 80 feet from where it was positioned.

Servicemen from the Illinois Valley witnessed the detonation on May 1, 1952. DoD photo.

A ROBINSON CRUSOE STORY

Few details about individual soldiers fighting in Korea were revealed by the military for security reasons. Battlefield reports consisted mainly of general news items about dogfights in MiG alley, bombing raids on North Korean staging areas or the hill fighting around places like Bunker Hill, Old Baldy, and T-Bone Hill. However, one pilot from Ottawa had gained some notoriety. On Feb. 19, USAF Col. Albert Schinz was featured in the Republican Times for downing his first MiG in an engagement between 26 F-86s and 50 MiGs in MiG alley.

In May, Lorraine Schinz, his wife, learned that her husband was missing in action in Korea; few details were available. A month later, she received a phone call at 4:20 a.m. from Tusiki, Japan. It was her husband. In a brief conversation with his wife and young daughter, the colonel told her he would be returning to Ottawa very soon.

Once back in the U.S., Schinz boarded a Rock Island train and on June 19, arrived in Ottawa at noon. He was greeted by hundreds of well-wishers at the depot and was amazed at the hero's welcome he received. On hand were his wife and two children, Penny, age 4, and Fritz, age 2. The hugs, kisses, and handshakes from those at the station marked just the beginning of a warm welcome. A parade of cars and the American Legion Corvets headed down LaSalle Street. Arriving at Columbus Street, the crowd formed into a square, where "Semper Fidelis" was played in his honor. The next day he said, "I have never been so honored and flattered in all my life."

Although local reporters tried their best to find out the details of his experience, he could only reveal a few facts concerning his disappearance. On May 1, while he was on a mission with the 51st Fighter Interceptor Wing, He had been engaged in a brief dogfight with some MiGs. "I didn't hold my break long enough. One of them got lucky and tagged me." His F-86 Saber jet was shot down behind enemy lines. He had little to eat for 37 days; grew a beard; and ended up cutting his own hair. Beyond that, Schinz would say nothing.

Col. Albert Schinz continued to command Air Force units in the Korean War and the Vietnam War. He was eventually promoted to Major General. Photo contributed by Robert Schinz.

The details of Schinz's survival on a deserted North Korean island were finally revealed in a Life magazine story by Clair Blair Jr. dated July 28, 1952. Entitled "Robinson Crusoe of Schinz-do," the article described how the Ottawa pilot's F-86 was hit by a 37-mm shell from a pursuing MiG while flying along the Yalu River. He was able to eject and parachute safely into the water near an uninhabited island on the northwest coast of the Korean peninsula. Schinz managed to paddle ashore in his life raft, but quickly found his emergency radio was broken. He only had a small signal mirror in his survival

gear to attract any rescue plane that might fly over his position. The island had been abandoned for many months, so he could reconnoiter the island without fear of being captured. He initially built a lean-to for cover and then tried to find some food. He survived on a diet consisting mostly of onions, corn, and dandelion greens. He tried fishing but without luck. It was going to be a very long 37-day ordeal. The story went on to say he tried to attract attention by using a supply of cotton he found in the village to spell out SOS. However, the crew of a B-26, that repeatedly flew overhead, failed to respond to his distress signal. Later during his ordeal, he spelled out MAY DAY on the ground, but again there was no apparent result.

Col. Schinz grew discouraged as a B-26 like this one flew over his position. The crew did not indicate any response to his signal for help. USAF photo.

In reality, the Air Rescue Service was aware that someone was on the island, but a rescue mission was postponed for fear that it might be a North Korean trap. Schinz was finally discovered by a group of South Koreans passing the island in their sampan and stopped to invesitgate; planning to kill any North Koreans who might have decided to occupy the island. They were happy to discover the person on the island was an American pilot and took him to safety.

Only a few American pilots who were shot down were able to avoid capture and escape back to their units. Schinz's tale of survival was among the most notable during the entire war.

GRANVILLE'S EYE IN THE SKY

One pilot from Granville, Capt. Bud Donaldson, was a veteran of WWII, where he was awarded a Silver Star for his many misisons flying an observation plane over Japanese positions. When the Korean War broke out in June 1950, he received orders to report for duty once again. He was assigned to the 7th Infantry Division. Rather than train younger pilots in light planes, he chose to fly an unarmed helicopter at tree-top level to spot enemy positions.

Capt. Donaldson (at left) was congratulated after completing his 40th misison by Capt. Herbert H. Eger of El Paso, TX. Both men had flown together in missions during WWII in the Pacific. After flying 40 combat missions, Donaldson was awarded the Air Medal. US Army photo published on Jan. 20. Photo contributed by Dorothy Donaldson.

READY FOR RUSSIAN BOMBERS

There was increasing fear of a Soviet attack on America. On Monday, July 14, the Ground Observation Corps began its participation in Operation Skywatch. The orders for activation of the 320 observation posts in northern Illinois came from the Air Defense Command in Washington, D.C. Each unit in Illinois was part of a checkerboard pattern of posts located about eight miles apart.

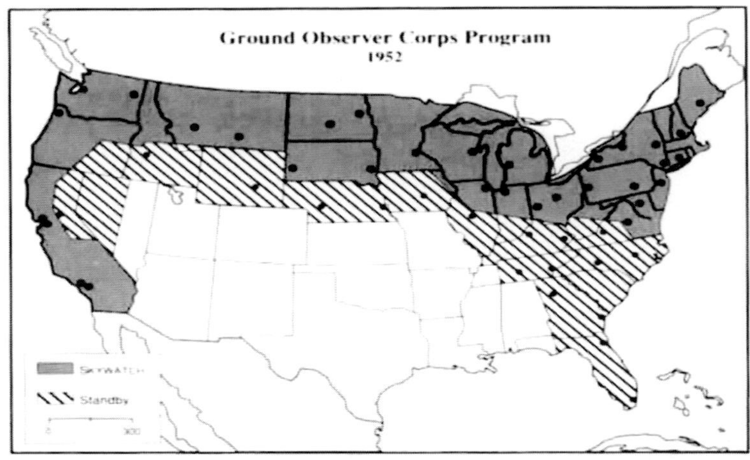

This map shows the area in which the USAF felt it was necessary to use ground observers to fill in the gaps of the fledgling radar system. In an age before ICBM's, the fear persisted that low-flying Soviet bombers could fly over the pole and drop nuclear weapons on American cities.

Only the northern part of Illinois had an active GOC. The southern units coordinated by Springfield were inactive. GOC spotters in Granville at the Hopkins H.S., were among the 10,000 observers, who were issued silver wings after 50

hours of service. Volunteers worked in pairs on a two-hour rotating basis, 24-hours a day. Julius Hansen, the Granville supervisor, called for more volunteers to join his group since this was more than a weekend drill. Mrs. Corrine Eckerd was one of those volunteers, who, almost 60 years later, still recalled standing in the field with a pair of binoculars watching the skies over Granville with her husband Edwin, and another couple.

THE FLYING SAUCER MANIA

Others saw a threat from aliens in flying saucers. Later that summer, several Ottawa residents reported sightings of brilliant lights in the sky. Mrs. Russell Daugherty reported a sighting 12 miles north of Ottawa. On July 14, she told the Republican Times she was watching from her yard on Saturday night around 9 p.m. "It appeared to be oblong, and there was a yellowish mist around it. Then it changed to the shape of a disc, I am certain it wasn't a plane. There was no sound. It came from the east and moved in a southwesterly direction. The object was visible for less than 30 seconds and then it was gone. We saw no further trace of it," Mrs. Daugherty said,

Mr. and Mrs. Don Nardon and their children gave a similar description to the Times. They observed the lights moving across the sky while driving down Rt. 71 from Chicago around 6:30 p.m. on Thursday, July 10. They were about 40 miles northeast of Ottawa at the time of the sighting.

Mr. and Mrs. W. H. Fisher were driving on Highway 23 north of Ottawa on July 14, when they observed a "greenish silver light shaped like a ball" at exactly 9:05 p.m. Mr. Fisher described the incident for the Ottawa Times. "It appeared to be traveling at two or three times the speed of a transport airplane. It came from the east and was headed in a straight westerly direction My impression was that the bright, greenish color resembled a mercury vapor light. It was very brilliant for a period of about 30 seconds, and then suddenly disappeared. It seemed to be about three or four miles away at the time I saw it. There was no sound that could be heard."

Another observer was Mrs. Charles Benjamin, who was seated in her car at the home of her daughter, Mrs. Dorothy Vezain. Her six-year old grandson, Marvin Vezain, was seated next to her in the car. He also saw the object. She said it appeared as two ovals combined. "The front part was very bright. I never saw anything like it before. It was visible for a period of about eight seconds, then seemed to pass under a cloud, although I could see nothing in the sky that looked like a cloud. Then it reappeared, very dimly, for a moment. "It seemed to be about the size of the moon when high in the sky."

Mr. and Mrs. Matthew J. Dekreon, Miss Dorothy Clause, and Henry Hoffman of LaSalle all reported a sighting of a light looking "like a white tongue of fire" while they were at Illini State Park near Marseilles. Mr. Dekreon, a former pilot, estimated the object to be flying at about 10,000 feet in a southwesterly direction. He said, "It was hard to judge though." Mrs. Dekreon said it was broader at the front and larger than any star. As it traveled across the sky, "It seemed to leave a trail of red sparks." One might speculate that the object they were all watching was nothing more than a fireball.

Perhaps sightings like these had a very plausible explanation. However, on July 22, the Republican Times also reported incidents of flying saucers over the nation's capital by credible witnesses. Air traffic controllers at Washington National Airport followed eight unidentified targets traveling 100-130 mph. near Andrews AFB. C. S. Casey Pierman, the pilot of Capitol Airlines flight 807 flying from National Airport, also reported seven objects between Washington and Marinsburg, W. VA. The pilot of Capital National Airlines flight 610 reported a light following his plane to within four miles of the capital. One fighter jet that happened to be in the vicinity could not close with the "steady white lights" even though his speed was 600 mph. Eight to twelve radar targets continued to appear from 1 a.m. until 6 a.m.

One would think the unidentified objects so close to the capital would have been serious enough to alert the Air Defense Command. When the CAA was asked why they didn't notify the USAF, a CAA official replied in an offhanded manner, "We were too busy with other things, and besides, those objects aren't hurting anybody."

At the end of July, the Air Force tried to explain the sightings of flying saucers, which were numbering about 100 a month over the country. According to the Air Force, they were nothing more than summertime temperature inversions, which caused objects, such as car headlights and streetlights, to be reflected upward and appear as objects in the sky.

That explanation didn't stop UFO reports. On Oct. 29, James Potter and John Prince, USAF inspectors at the Eicor plant in Oglesby, observed a "saucer" at 4:25 p.m. hovering over LaSalle. Potter, a former radar operator with the USAF, filed a report with officials at Wright Patterson AFB in Ohio, the command center for "Operation Saucer," which investigated UFO claims. He said they spotted the bright elliptical object as they approached Shippingsport Bridge on their way home from work. The sausage-shaped object disappeared after accelerating to a "terrific rate" in a northwesterly direction. Potter said he was certain the object was not any aircraft with which he was familiar. There were over 1,500 sightings in 1952, the highest number in the Air Force's 21-year investigation of UFO's.

One major problem faced by the Air Force was finding enough GOC volunteers to man the lookout towers, which sprang up across the country. At left is a stamp used by the USAF to recruit civilians for the GOC.

On July 12, President Truman personally appealed for citizens to join the GOC. There was still a need for 350,000 volunteers to maintain a 24-hr Skywatch program. On July 24, Capt. Edward Ruppelt of Project Blue Book, the USAF file on UFO's, emphatically stated that Operation Skywatch had nothing to do with the large number of sightings of UFO's. However, after a second wave of UFO sightings in July, more volunteers joined the GOC, and Air Force enlistments dramatically increased.

Looking back on the phenomenon, many questions are still unanswered. Was there a correlation between the lack of volunteers in the Skywatch program and the rash of UFO sightings? Were the UFO reports faked as a ploy to entice more volunteers to join the GOC program? The GOC volunteers continued their mission until the program was cancelled in 1959. It should be noted UFO sightings still continue in 2010.

A SUMMER OF CELEBRATIONS

Major events during the summer of '52 included a number of anniversary celebrations. In June, Oglesby celebrated its Golden Jubilee. The 50th anniversary festivities began on Thursday, June 12 and continued through the weekend. Introductory remarks were made by General Chairman John McCann, Mayor Burton Mayers, and Frank Moyle, vice president of Marquette Cement. Entertainment began with Frank Grubar calling the sets for the Twirling Teens, who square danced to the music of the Eikens Trio from Amboy. Other notable entertainers included Patsy Montana and Bob Archer, stars of the WLS National Barn Dance program. The Oglesby municipal band held a concert at Dickinson Field in the evening.

In spite of the Friday the 13th rainstorm that blew down the Oglesby program tent and drenched and damaged floats with 1.62 inches of rain, the parade was held as scheduled. Oglesby library collection.

Parade photo from Oglesby library collection.

On Sunday at 2 p.m., the Oglesby police and fire department vehicles and those from Mark and Utica led the marching units and floats in the parade down the street lined by a crowd estimated at 25,000. Marching units came from local groups as well as Kankakee and Chicago. Old timers rode in a carriage and a stagecoach. City officials from the Tri-Cities as well as Streator, Spring Valley, Tonica, Lostant, Rutland, Mendota, and Utica joined in the parade.

The next major summer event was the LaSalle Centennial on July 31-Aug. 3. The official opening of activities was heralded by the explosion of aerial bombs, ringing of church bells, and the sounds of factory whistles and city sirens. A style show was held at the Kaskaskia Hotel, and the Spring Valley band played in the evening at First and Gooding Streets. Urbino's 50-piece Swing Accordion band performed in the afternoon. Activities continued at the L-P H.S. stadium.

After formal remarks by Centennial General Manager Stuart Duncan, the L-P High School band held a concert and performed a variety of marching formations on the football field. One formation depicted an old coalmine and dump in keeping the historical nature of the celebration. The Friday night celebration concluded with a gigantic fireworks finale.

The LP band formed into a coalmine tipple with a slag pile.

Homecoming Day offered an opportunity for the children to march in their own parade. LaSalle library photos.

Saturday's main activities included a concert by the Peru Municipal band; platform and aerial acts; a banquet at the Kaskaskia Hotel; an evening concert by the Oglesby Municipal Band; and a street dance from 9 p.m. until midnight.

The Parade of the Century drew a crowd estimated at over 50,000 persons. It took over three hours for the 225 military and civilian marching units, bands, and floats from cities near and far, to pass the reviewing stand. The parade stretched for a distance of five miles.

Churches, businesses, civic groups, cities, and commercial floats together with military marching units and veterans groups fell into line as the parade kicked off at 2 p.m.

Every town in the area seemed to have a float. Ottawa was represented by a city float and car. The 45-piece high school band led by Majorette Mabel Beguin marched with the school drill team. Naplate also entered an official car and float. Three units represented Putnam County. Granville's Legion Post 180 entered its famous "mule" with Fritz Ballerine, Bud Donaldson, and Don Hynds at the controls. Bruno Biagi and Leo Donini rode in Mark's horse-drawn surrey. Riders from the Hennepin Saddle Club included Carl Nelson, his son, Charles, and his grandson, Gayland. Norma Zellmer rode with them.

LaSalle's famous gambling establishment, Kelley and Cawley's, entered this unit in the Centennial Parade.

The LaSalle National Bank received the first place trophy, and the LaSalle city float carried the queen and her attendants. LaSalle Library photos.

The L-P H.S. band was one of the largest ones in the parade.
LaSalle library photo.

There were many other festivities in the summer of '52. The Spring Valley Boat Club sponsored the Tommy Bartlett Water Show. On Aug. 8-10, there were five performances of ski jumping, clown acts, and boat jumping on the Illinois River east of the Route 89 bridge.

Mendota held its fifth annual Sweet Corn Festival in August. On August 12, a parade, featuring 35 floats, cars, and trucks, made its way downtown. The Sweet Corn Queen, 17-year old Carol Loach from West Brooklyn, rode on the royal float with her attendants, Marjorie Boyle and Donna Mosher. The Mendota Hospital Auxiliary float was best in its class. In another category, the VFW auxiliary won a first place award. In the children's parade, Ronnie Sessler (at right), son of Mr. and Mrs. Oscar Sessler of Mendota was awarded first place with his wagon carrying a duck and a pot of roasting ears. The next

day, an estimated crowd of 20,000 residents and visitors enjoyed over seven tons of hot-buttered sweet corn.

THE DAY THE GENERAL CAME TO OTTAWA

There seemed to be no end to the cheering in 1952. On Sept. 15, the city turned out to welcome Dwight Eisenhower, who was campaigning as the Republican candidate for the presidency. Every adult remembered the former general's reputation as the D-Day commander in WWII so the gathering

was more than political. Ike made stops in Joliet, Wheaton, and Aurora, where he was greeted by a crowd of 45,000. Thousands more lined Rt. 71 hoping for a view of the presidential candidate as his 50-car motorcade traveled from Aurora to Ottawa. Residents from Yorkville and Newark lined the road with "I Like Ike" banners. Even the towns' fire engines were parked next to the highway. Farm families turned on yard lights and sat around bonfires waiting for the caravan.

Police sirens began wailing to signal the arrival of the general at the city park in Ottawa at 9:25 p.m. A crowd of 15,000 watched Ottawa mayor Phil Bailey present Ike with the key to the city. The cheering of the general was compared to the excitement of the Lincoln-Douglas debate in 1858.

In his speech, Eisenhower spoke only briefly about the Korean War and international relations. He focused instead on the economy and called for an end to high prices and high taxes. "How much will your dollar buy now compared to 1940?" he asked the crowd. He also derided corrupt politicians and called for the election of qualified public officials, who were devoted to the service of the people. He promised to change the government regulation of farmers, schools, and the economy and a return to decentralized power.

The stop in Ottawa was his last speaking engagement that day. Ike was due in Rock Island in the evening, but a small group waited in LaSalle hoping for a glimpse of the general.

UTICA CELEBRATES 100 YEARS

Utica also had cause to celebrate. During Oct. 17-19, residents observed their centennial. Events began with aerial bombs exploding and sirens wailing on Friday night followed by formal remarks by Mayor John Kidd. The Joe DeZutti Orchestra played for the street dance that continued until midnight. The children's parade was the next day. A WLS musical show, a six-act historical pageant, and a square dance rounded out the major activities.

On Sunday, traffic was backed up to Rt. 6 as thousands tried to find parking in the village while the floats lined up for the parade. Strong fall winds delayed the start of the parade for 45 minutes while repairs were hastily made to wind-damaged floats. A cannon blast signaled the start of the parade. The Legion jeep led the way. It took an hour and a half for the 85 marching units and floats to complete the two-mile parade route and finally pass in review on Mill Street. Businesses, churches, civic groups, and military

organizations entered floats. James Bray and Peggy Carey rode in the parade as king and queen. The junior royal family riding on the Junior Women's float included Holly Kehle and Jackie Pelsynski.

Music for the Utica parade was provided by the Ottawa H.S. band, the L-P-O School Band, the Streator High School band, and the Tonica Concert Band.

Parade photos from the Utica library collection.

MIXED NEWS FROM KOREA

As the year came to an end, stories from the front lines of Korea tempered the joy of the previous months of celebrations. The election of Dwight Eisenhower held hope for a speedy end to the fighting that continued on such places as Triangle Hill, Sniper Ridge, and Jane Russell Hill.

The Illinois 44th Infantry was required to move from Camp Cooke to Ft. Lewis, WA. It was discovered the 84,000-acre training area in California was situated on top of an oil field owned by the Union Oil Co.

Other Illinois Valley men were returning to Seattle aboard the *Marine Adder*. Among the 2,800 men aboard the ship were Pfc. LaVerne K. Cast (Earlville), Sgt. Howard Turner (Wyanet), Cpl. Earl R. Davis (Sparland), Sgt. Lawrence Ogden (Sheridan), and Pfc. Lewis J. Panti (Marseilles).

Some Illinois Valley soldiers were coming home aboard the naval transport *Marine Adder* during the Korean War. US Navy photo.

Capt. Anthony J. Skotnicki of Peru was still in Korea, where he was awarded a second Bronze Star. He earned his first Bronze Star in the fighting at Iwo Jima in WWII. During the fighting in August, he distinguished himself while leading an infantry company of the First Marine Division. While under intense mortar and artillery fire for four days and nights, he directed the evacuation of casualties and moved into forward positions to direct artillery fire to repel enemy counter-attacks.

Most of the local men who served in Korea eventually made it home safely. However, many were wounded, and over 50 men from the area were killed. Pfc. Virgil C. Shelley Jr. from LaSalle was one of those who was killed in action. Although he was buried in August 1952, it was another year before his parents received a citation and medal from the Navy Department. The 19-year old marine was awarded the Silver Star posthumously. According to the citation, on July 3, 1952, Pfc. Shelley was "mortally wounded by hostile machinegun fire while covering his platoon during its movement to fresh positions."

Among the casualty reports in December was the news that Pvt. Harold Underwood, 19, of Peru was killed in action on Dec. 10. He and his twin brother, Howard, had been deployed with the 44th Infantry to Korea in December. His parents had just received a letter from Howard in which he said, "everything is fine."

Other news was inspiring. Second Lt. Fred Gray, a former Spring Valley Junior High teacher, who enlisted in the USAF in March 1951; became a fighter pilot; and was sent to Korea. On the day after Christmas, his former students learned from a letter to his wife that he been in a dogfight with a MiG. He told how he was low on fuel when a MiG started shooting at Calvin Davey, his group leader. A quick warning to Davey from Gray saved Davey. The MiG's cannon fire went under the plane as Davey pulled up. Lt. Gray fired his remaining ammunition and hit the MiG twice. Low on fuel, Gray turned back to his base to the south. "I got out okay," he said.

Gray was one of three pilots from Ottawa. He flew on several missions with Capt. C. Carr. Together they shot down a MiG, a month after Gray's close encounter. The other pilot from Ottawa was Col. Albert Schinz.

Another soldier from Spring Valley, M/Sgt. Edward J. Pizzamiglio, was reported missing in action, but after three days, he was released uninjured by his Communist captors on Dec. 30. He returned to the U.S. to give secret testimony in Washington, D.C. about his capture.

1953
THE DAY THEY CLOSED CAWLEY'S

Kelly-Cawley's new location on First Street in LaSalle.

Saturday, Feb. 21, 1953, marked the historic raid that would turn the "Little Reno" world of LaSalle casinos upside-down. A secret raid on Cawley's new establishment at 517 First Street had been planned with the knowledge of only a few people. At 3 p.m., State's Attorney Warren and the assistant state's attorney, Wendall Thompson, along with deputies Stanley Murray, David Monterastelli, Bernard Kleinhans, and investigator James Entwistle entered the cigar store portion of the building on the first floor. Kleinhans read the search warrant to William Brady, one of Cawley's clerks, while Thompson led the team to the second floor over the Senate portion of the building and a gambling room over the cigar portion. The horse-betting cage was open, and racing forms were scattered on the floor. Dealers and bartenders hurriedly tried to remove incriminating evidence of gambling activities.

Patrons were allowed to leave, but no one was allowed to enter the building until all of the gambling equipment was removed, which took two hours.

Warren personally answered the phone in the cashier's cage several times as eager bettors tried to make wagers on different races. The phones rang periodically with many of the callers wanting to know the results of the second race at Hialeah. Illinois Bell was notified to come to the business to take note of the kinds of calls being received.

The state's attorney answered the phone in the cashier's cage during the raid and gave the callers fictitious information about race results. By calling number 208 at Cawley's, an individual could learn the latest in racing results or place a bet. Photo by Bob Johns for the News-Tribune.

An instruction sign for craps shooters was taken down by Deputy Sheriff Stanley Murray.

Photo by Bob Johns for the News-Tribune on Feb. 23, 1953.

The raiders confiscated craps tables, a roulette table, 668 punchboards, 270 ticket boards, 68 jars, Peoria baseball pools, poker tables, cards, chips, racing forms, newspapers, and even match books with the copy indicating that racing results were available at Cawley's. The authorities also confiscated $77.80 on the poker tables, and $175 in the cashier's cage. According to Ryan Cawley, there was always $500 in the book drawer at the beginning of every day. For some reason, never explained, Ryan said only $20 actually got back to Ottawa that day. In any case, all the gambling equipment was loaded into trucks and taken back to Ottawa.

Pictured is the confiscated K-C roulette wheel, which was returned later to be used for amusement purposes only.
Tom Cawley II collection.
Photo by author.

Police logged in evidence confiscated during the raid. Ryan Cawley photo.

Brady, Tom Cawley, and his nephew, Ryan Cawley, were ordered to report to Ottawa for the formal reading of charges. Attorney Patrick Cawley, Tom Cawley's son, accompanied his father and Ryan to Ottawa. A $2,000 bond was required of each of the accused for their release. Tom Cawley's personal check was refused, as was a property bond. The banks were closed, and Washington's birthday on Feb. 22 would mean a bank holiday on the following Monday. If the gambling czar did not come up with the money, he would have to spend the three-day weekend in jail along with his nephew and Mr. Brady. Fortunately, a friend of the Cawley's in Ottawa came up with the bond money, and they were released.

Workers loaded the craps and roulette tables into a truck for the trip to the Ottawa police station where they would be stored pending a hearing on Mar. 2, 1953.
News-Tribune photo.

Warren went to Mayor Bildhauer, who was also the liquor commissioner, and asked for the revocation of the liquor license at the Senate tavern. The mayor refused saying, "The charge was not serious enough." He added, "I see no reason why the tavern should be closed, employees thrown out of a job, and a person made to lose a business in which thousands of dollars are invested."

Taylor Wilhelm, a former LaSalle State's attorney, was employed by Tom Cawley to defend him against the charges. He argued that the case should be dismissed. The former LaSalle state's attorney also explained why he never went after the gamblers as an enforcement officer of the legal system. Directing his remarks to Warren, he said, "You don't want to prosecute; you only wish to persecute." He also demanded that Warren take the witness stand. "You (Warren) were there as a raider, hence you must testify as a raider!" Warren, who did not wish to take the stand, was upset by the inflammatory tactics. The judge granted the defense a continuance until Mar. 23 and reduced the defendant's bond to $1,000.

In the meantime, other action was being taken against Cawley. A week had passed, and the phone company decided to disconnect the phones at the 517 First Street location. The excuse was they were being used for illegal purposes. Pat

Cawley was denied a motion to have an injunction issued to restrain Illinois Bell.

Grand jury indictments against Cawley were handed down on Mar. 19. The charges were bookmaking; having gambling equipment on the premises; selling alcohol without a license; and operating gambling equipment. Five members of the Cawley family were named in the indictments. Two other individuals were indicted: William Brady, a clerk at the casino: and Vincent Flannery, the manager of the Senate tavern located on the first floor of the Kelly-Cawley building. Flannery was also the manager of the Lincoln Tavern formerly managed by Jimmy Keys for Tom Cawley. Numerous witnesses had been called before the grand jury including Bildhauer, Police Chief Kasprowicz, telephone company workers, Cawley employees, a member of the Illinois liquor commission, and several "ticket" distributors.

The case began in late May. Judge William Hibbs, the same man who had closed down Cawley's casino at 621 First Street in 1952, was the trial judge in the latest hearing. Howard Ryan, an attorney from Tonica, assisted Warren for the prosecution.

Warren began his testimony by describing the raid. Proceeding up the back stairs, they saw ten men who were trying to exit the building, but, as soon as the police were spotted, they ran back inside the building. Then a call went to the LaSalle County jail for all available officers to converge on Cawley's. When the deputy sheriffs arrived, they proceeded to the second floor where they found John Cawley. Warren then called for a truck and checked on the progress of the officers on the first floor as they collected punchboards.

On May 21, deputy sheriff Bernard Kleinhans took the stand to identify the tickets, which were confiscated from the lucky jars. Warren also described how the phone rang constantly with individuals who wanted the latest results from various racetracks.

The following day, defense attorney Wilhelm questioned Wendell Thompson about Tom Cawley's reactions during the Feb. 21 raid. The attorney said that Tom had just been standing there and spoke briefly to one of the police officers saying, "What are you trying to do to me?" The officer only shrugged his shoulders and said, "We were drafted." Then Cawley answered the phone. He told the unidentified caller, "They're taking everything away from us except the building." Wilhelm also tried to show that Ryan Cawley really wasn't involved in gambling activities when the police were there.

Judge Hibbs scheduled further testimony for June 22. When the hearing resumed, the state's attorney decided to drop all charges against Elizabeth Cawley.

The case against the Cawley family dragged on into the fall. In September, the defendants were ordered to pay $8,000. Part of the deal to avoid any prison time was to promise to get out of the gambling business.

The Cawleys still had 150 slot machines stored in a building on their farm in rural Dimmick. What would they do with all those slot machines? According to Ryan Cawley, a man from England met with his uncle several times before an agreement was reached. The slots were all sold for only $100 apiece. One day, some trucks from Quesse Transfer backed up to the warehouse in Dimmick and loaded them to take to Chicago where they would be loaded on a train and eventually, sent by ship to England. Ironically, the US Coast Guard seized all the machines before they left the country.

The Cawley casino in LaSalle was closed. It had been a major gathering spot not only for gamblers but also for ordinary people out for an evening of dining and entertainment.

With the closure of Kelly and Cawley's, the other casinos soon followed suit. It would not bring an end to all gambling in the Illinois Valley. That never really ended. It was just an end to a quarter century of dominance by Tom Cawley. Recalling that fateful day over 50 years ago, Bob Hobneck of Tonica said, "It was a big disappointment. They were good people."

In 2004, Ryan Cawley looked back on those years and said, "I was always amazed at the people from Rockford,

Peoria, Chicago, and Joliet. They would come in one weekend; stay at Starved Rock; enjoy the entertainment, gambling, and fun. We never thought what we did was illegal."

Right: Painting of Tom Cawley from Tom Cawley II.
Far right: Ryan Cawley left the gambling business to establish a LaSalle real estate firm.

FIRE TAKES A TOLL AT ST. BEDE

While the closing of Kelly-Cawley was a major event in LaSalle, a fire at St. Bede on March 9 was an alarming disaster in Peru. Fighting the blaze, which was discovered at 12:40 a.m. by Valentine Valens, one of the janitors, was made all the more difficult by the 13° temperature. Flames were burning through the roof when fire departments from Spring Valley and Peru arrived. Four explosions occurred while the firemen were inspecting the inside corridors. Those explosions coupled with the intense heat melted the girders supporting the roof and caused the walls and roof to collapse. The gym, which had the largest playing floor in the Tri-City area, was built in 1926 at a cost of $250,000. By Monday morning, all that remained of the gym was the front wall with the entrance and a weakened south wall.

This was not the first time St. Bede had a major fire. On May 27, 1945, a fire broke out in the attic and damaged the third floor to such an extent that academic studies were cancelled for the remainder of the school year. Fortunately, the damage was limited to $50,000, and the museum was saved.

The immediate concern in the athletic department was the status of the IV Frosh Basketball Tourney. The Bruins had just beat Marseilles 51-22 and Hall 41-33 to make it to the title round. Howard Fellows, the L-P athletic director, offered the use of the L-P gym so the St. Bede boys could practice before the game against Ottawa.

The boys were successful in winning the tournament by beating Ottawa 38-25 in the Kingman Gym. There remained the daunting job of replacing the gym. Initial estimates placed the cost at $500,000. When the bids were opened in April 1954, they were over the engineer's estimate by $150,000, an amount too large for the religious community to accept even with the insurance reimbursement. However, with some revisions the costs were reduced by $90,000 making it affordable. The planned bowling alley in the basement would have to wait, but otherwise, much of the structure would be included as planned.

The new gym pictured with the entrance to the old St. Vincent's gym at right was completed in time for the June 5, 1955 graduation ceremonies. Photo by author.

CORN'S ROLE IN THE COLD WAR

Hardly anyone would consider local seed companies to be instrumental in stopping communism, but in February, an effort was taken in that direction. The Moews Seed Co. in Granville, working with 16 other seed-growing companies in Illinois, teamed up to participate in CROP, the Christian Rural Overseas Program. Over 2,000 rural villages in northern Greece were devastated by the war with the communists. Their buildings were burned, and livestock was stolen. To assist in the CROP, Warren Moews, assistant manager at Moews Seed, Jim Tonarelli, Earl Boone, and Darrell Alleman loaded Moews seed corn into a boxcar at the IC depot in LaSalle. Then it was transported to an Atlantic Coast port for shipment to Greece.

INVASION, ILLINOIS?

All the attention given to civil defense in 1952 and 1953 was warranted by new developments in the Soviet Air Force. Their prototype Tu-85 Barge bombers, which were copies of the American B-29, had a range of over 7,000 miles, making the Soviet bombers intercontinental threats. The Soviets improved the Tu-85 and introduced their faster Tu-95 Bear bomber (below) in 1952. With an unrefueled range of 9,400 miles, this was the plane the USAF feared would be used in an attack on the United States. To counter this possibility, Operation Skywatch was expanded.

The Air Force decided more ground observers were needed in the Illinois Valley. A meeting was held on April 15 at the American Legion Hall in Ottawa. Lt. T. L. Wilson of the Air Defense Command used a film entitled "One Plane, One Bomb, One City" to illustrate the importance of civilian participation in the GOC. The officer described the need for an observation post as "imperative."

Illinois Valley movie patrons saw a Hollywood version of a nuclear attack in "Invasion, USA." News-Tribune ad - Mar. 17, 1953.

The scenario depicted in the Air Force film was an invasion of Soviet bombers flying over Illinois to attack industrial targets in Joliet and Chicago. Lt. Wilson called for 84 volunteers and said, "This is your opportunity to earn Air Force Wings and do your country a vital service." Unfortunately, only 20 potential volunteers attended, and half of them were high school students.

In Peru, Casimir Chamlin, civil defense coordinator, and John O'Hearn, the observation post supervisor, announced a similar meeting for April 16 at St. Joseph's Hall. Plans called for a post to be constructed on top of the municipal building on Fourth Street in Peru. They hoped to have it operating by the first week in May.

Almost weekly, the newspapers were filled with stories of atomic bomb testing in Nevada. On Mar. 17, Pfc. John Mitchell, the son of Wilma Eickelkraut of Utica, was one of the 1,000 soldiers and hundreds of civilian spectators watching Test Annie in the Upshot-Knothole series of detonations. In this experiment, the government wanted to learn the effects of a nuclear explosion on houses and cars.

The nuclear device, codenamed XR3, was mounted on a 300-foot tower. Two combat brigades and 20 reporters were within two miles of the 16-kiloton blast. It was 5:30 a.m. when the shockwave hit and the purplish-red fireball rose above Area 3. People in La Vegas could see the glow in the sky 75 miles away. US govt. photo.

EXCHANGE OF WOUNDED POWS

The threat of a war with the Soviets was tempered by steps toward peace in Korea. The fighting would claim fewer lives of soldiers from the Illinois Valley in 1953. Among the seven men who died was Pfc. Jack Shanyfelt of Mendota, who was killed on Feb. 22 as a member of the 1st Marine Division fighting at the Western Outposts. Another marine, Pfc. Ray Szymovicz from Peru, was killed in the same area on Mar. 28.

The end of the fighting was approaching in small steps. A "peace village" was established at Munson, Korea, where there would soon be an exchange of wounded POW's in Operation Little Switch. The process of repatriation was described in a letter from Sgt. Don Kostellic to his parents in Granville. He was serving with the Army's Ground Casualty Division in the spring of 1953. On April 19, his detachment left Seoul in a convoy of two jeeps and one 6 x 6 truck. Traveling the dusty road to Freedom Village at Munson, the trip took 2 hours and 45 minutes. After a meal, they had a final briefing before the exchange of POWs the next day.

The processing tent described by Sgt. Kostellic for repatriated Americans at Munson. Department of Defense photo.

The next morning, April 20, was rainy, but at least that settled the dust on the roads. A large sign had been erected in front of each of the four processing tents, "Welcome – Gate to Freedom." A small UN flag was attached to one signpost along with another flag on the other post indicating the processing locations for American litter patients, American ambulatory personnel, British soldiers, and one for other UN allies. In addition to American officers awaiting the exchange of prisoners, there were also officers from Great Britain, Turkey, Colombia, Greece, Canada, South Africa, Holland, and other UN allies.

When the North Korean ambulances arrived at 9 a.m., Gen. Mark Clark and Gen. Taylor greeted the first returnees. Processing each man consisted of spraying him with DDT followed by a medical checkup. Kostellic's unit handled the paperwork insuring that all vital information was accurately noted. The returning men were all dressed in clean, blue, quilted two-piece suits with blue tennis shoes. Their bandages and splints also appeared to be new. Outwardly, in Kostellic's opinion, they appeared to be well fed. Although some sat quietly, others were more talkative. All of the men seemed to be happy to be free from their captivity. Each man was interviewed; given a change of clothes; and evacuated by helicopter to a hospital at the rear. From there, the freed POWs were sent to Japan. By 1:30 p.m., Kostellic's unit had processed 50 men. The information they gathered was radioed back to the Dept. of the Army in Washington, D.C.

With occasional artillery fire in the distance, there was a chill in the air while Kostellic's men awaited the second group of POW's the following day. Everything was pretty much the same as the previous morning with one interesting addition. Just before they were released, some of the prisoners had been given a going away present, a bottle of Chinese liquor. During the first two days of repatriation, a hundred soldiers were turned over to the UN. Sixty of them were Americans; the rest were mostly British.

The following day, another 50 prisoners were expected. When they arrived, Kostellic learned that they were all South Koreans, who were processed separately.

On April 23, only 25 prisoners were released: 14 Americans, 6 Australians, and 5 Colombians. It was a slow, agonizing process. They hoped 40 POWs would be released the following day. One mishap, the crash of a helicopter carrying freed South Korean soldiers, concerned Kostellic and the other men until they learned there were no casualties.

Kostellic wrote that the Communists had released the number of POWs as they had promised although the numbers varied a little each day. When he had time, he talked to the returnees and learned that the British POWs were given better treatment than that afforded to the Americans. He thought that might have been because England had formally recognized Red China, but the United States did not.

Not all of the men were in good physical condition. One in particular caught Kostellic's attention. "He had half-healed wounds, but the guy was as thin as anyone I have ever seen. Nothing but skin tightly drawn over bones. He was well photographed, but did not speak to the press," Kostellic wrote.

Lt. Fred W. Gray had completed 88 missions and served as a test pilot after that. While home on a furlough in April, he was interviewed by a News-Tribune reporter, who asked about the differences between MiGs and Sabre Jets. Lt. Gray praised the Russian MiG and said it was superior to the F-86 in several ways especially at altitudes above 30,000 feet. However, he added, "We've been successful against them only because of superior training." The WWII veteran also said that the MiGs usually outnumbered the Saber Jets, but "they are just as likely to run as they are to give battle."

F-86 Sabre Jet flying over Korea in 1953. USAF photo.

In spite of the exchange of wounded soldiers, thousands of men remained in POW camps on both sides, and the fighting continued. The News-Tribune reported on May 13 Sgt. Edward Mrowicki from LaSalle was awarded a Bronze Star during his second tour of duty in Korea with the Marines. He was serving with a marine tank battalion reconnaissance section and participated in 25 patrols. On some of these occasions, he moved through enemy minefields and was under fire while obtaining tactical information of enemy positions. For his devotion to duty and contribution of vital information, he was awarded the Bronze Star with the combat "V."

On June 11, the communists launched their greatest drive since the 1951 spring offensive. They drove two miles deep into the UN-ROK line attacking Capitol Hill and Outpost Texas. Allied commanders felt this was their attempt to score one last victory before the truce, which was finally agreed to in late July. The negotiators had been working on the armistice document for over two years, but the signing ceremony on July 27 took little more than ten minutes.

One of the men who did not live to see the truce was 2nd Lt. Joe Cerri Jr. from Cedar Point. He was assigned to the 65th Infantry Regiment 3rd Infantry Division. On June 11, his platoon was under an artillery and mortar barrage followed by a ground assault by a numerically superior force at Kumhwa, N.K. Cerri was wounded by grenade fragments and fell into the path of the enemy onslaught. He kept firing until he lost consciousness and was dragged back to the enemy lines where he died. He was  posthumously awarded the Army's Distinguished Service Cross, the second highest decoration for gallantry in combat.

One casualty from Streator was 2nd Lt. Wallace R. Metz. On June 23, he was flying a C-119 ferrying soldiers from the 187th Airborne Regimental Combat Team when the plane crashed in the sea near Tsukishima Island.

Lt. Wallace Metz. Korean War Project photo.

Seven servicemen from the area were killed in 1953. Among that number was Pvt. Willard V. Norwick from rural Mendota was assigned to the 14th Inf. Reg. 25th Div. when he was killed on July 8, 1953. Another local soldier, Pfc. Charles E. Bergland, an assistant squad leader, was wounded. While recovering in a Tokyo hospital, he received his Purple Heart medal from his commander. His wife was living in Wyanet.

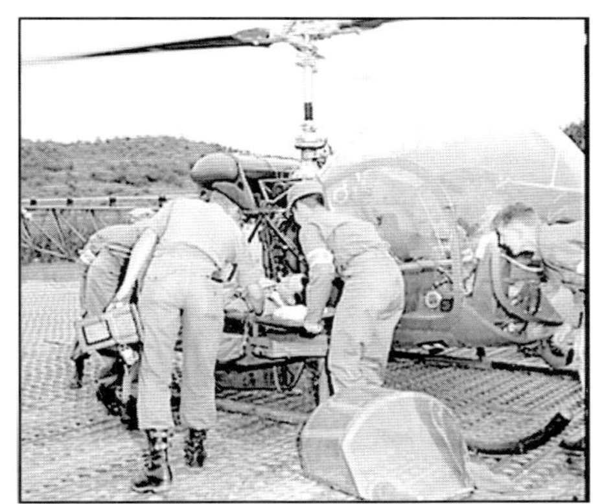

A badly wounded soldier was about to be flown out from Munson on Aug. 5, 1953. DoD photo. Not all of the POWs survived the rigors of confinement. According to DoD records, Cpl. Roy C. Johnson from Harding, IL was the only soldier from LaSalle County who died while held captive.

328 American POW's were among those sent home on the *Gen. Nelson M. Walker.* US Navy photo.

Many Korean War veterans received medals for heroic and conspicuous service. Cpl. Philip D. Kerz, whose parents moved from LaSalle to Dixon, was promoted to sergeant and awarded a Bronze Star for action on Feb. 3, 1953. The radioman was wounded in a company raid on an enemy hill but continued to send messages to his commander until he was evacuated. Another Bronze Star was awarded to 1st Lt. William

121

Etzenbach of Peru, who was a platoon leader in the 89th Tank Battalion,

A section of the veterans' memorial in Ottawa lists the local men who died in Korea. Note: A list of Illinois soldiers, who died in Korea, can be found at http://www.archives.gov/research/korean-war/casualty-lists/il-by-town.html.

KOREA

COSTELLO, JAMES
FINCH, WAYNE R.
GALLI, ARMAND J.
HAM, RUSSELL B. Jr.
JOHNSON, ROY C.
KNUTSON, FLOYD V.
MYERS, HARRY F.

Sgt. Floyd Davis of Wedron was the lone survivor of his tank group. All of his buddies were killed, and Davis was taken prisoner by the Chinese. In the first six months of captivity, his weight had dropped from 185 pounds to about 95 pounds. Although letters were exchanged during his captivity, he had to write he was receiving good food. When he returned home, he was finally able to give a true account of life in the POW camp. He said that conditions in the camp improved after the POW exchange was announced. Once in American hands, he was able to write home, "It is sure good to be eating American chow for a change instead of eating hog slop for over two years." He returned to Wedron on Sept. 16. Many more solders, marines, airmen, and sailors began coming home in the fall of 1953.

EYEWITNESS TO ATOMIC ANNIE

While the fighting in Korea dragged on, the Army continued to conduct tests of atomic bombs in Nevada. Several tests involved a tactical nuclear bomb that could be used on the battlefield. One new device was the atomic cannon, nicknamed "Atomic Annie." In May, Pfc. Gerald Konetshny, a fire direction specialist in Battery A of the 867th Field Artillery Battalion, was one of the 3,000 soldiers at Camp Desert Rock, NV, who witnessed the first test-firing of the weapon with a nuclear projectile. The LaSalle native had participated in the firing of the cannon with conventional shells. During the test of the nuclear projectile, the men crouched down behind an embankment 4,500 yards from the cannon at the Frenchman Flat test site when the 11-inch shell was fired. It exploded at a distance of about seven miles from the cannon. This would be the only time Konetshny would ever see such a blast again. The M65 cannon was never fired again with a nuclear projectile.

The result of the "Atomic Annie" nuclear test, code named Upshot-Knothole Test Grable, was an explosion measuring roughly 15 kilotons, similar to the bomb dropped over Hiroshima. National Nuclear Security Administration photo.

HEIDT IS BACK IN TOWN

Those servicemen from the Illinois Valley who witnessed a nuclear explosion would always remember the experience. On a much smaller scale of excitement, Horace Heidt, the radio star, was back in Peru in May to provide a different kind of personal thrill for a few individuals. After hearing about the talented 18-year old Ron Bozik from Peru, who won the talent contest at Ottawa H.S., Heidt decided to schedule the St. Bede senior to play his accordion in Wisconsin Rapids, WI for Heidt's Thursday night radio show, which was broadcast over WBBM. The crowd of 3,000 applauded several times during his rendition of "Twelfth Street Rag." Also on the program was a junior from Serena H.S., Delores Orsini, who sang "Love is Where You find It." Both received $25.

END OF THE LINE FOR THE H. Y. & T.

A more melancholy feeling was being experienced in western Bureau County. For 45 years, Bureau, Whiteside, and Henry counties shared the notoriety of having a section of tracks for the shortest railroad in Illinois. The Hooppole, Yorktown, and Tampico RR, a one-engine line, ran a mere 11.9 miles on a single track. There was no set schedule. Engineer Lee Groves simply ran it from one end of the tracks to the other. The company, headed by President Howard C. Mathis, only owned a 0-6-0 engine, a passenger car, a flat car, and a caboose. Boxcars were rented as necessary. Passenger service ended in 1929. The Depression killed off much of the line's business. No one even offered to buy it for $140, the amount Mathis needed just to pay the taxes. Running up a debt of $524 in 1951, the expenses became too much for the Mathis family. "You can't run a railroad on nostalgia – you've got to have revenue," said Mathis, who bought the railroad in 1910. The sporadic loads of lumber, coal, and grain barely generated enough money to pay for maintenance. In June 1953, the ICC authorized the railroad to suspend operations.

HY&T's No. 1315, a 0-6-0 engine at Hooppole, IL taking on coal on Aug. 13, 1941. The engine was acquired from the CB&Q in 1927. Photo from the William Raia collection.

ANOTHER SEASON OF CENTENNIALS

The summer of 1953 was noted for major celebrations. Ottawa celebrated its centennial for eight days, July 12-19. Each day had a specific theme: Agriculture Day, Industry and Labor Day, Ladies' Day, Old Settlers Day.

The first major event was the parade on Sunday afternoon where a crowd of 75,000 – the largest ever according to Police Chief Walter Keim – lined the route for 17 blocks. Parade marshal Ralph Woodward's car led the line of floats, bands, and cars. A treasure hunt for merchandise prizes followed. The crowning of centennial queen, Judy Harding, and Gerald Holm, King of the Bearded Brotherhood, was scheduled during the Centennial Ball at Kingman gym.

Other events during the centennial included a children's parade and Little League exhibition baseball. A Venetian Night parade of boats on the Illinois River and music festival closed out the day's events. The three-performances of the "Ottawa, USA" pageant featured a cast of 200 and starred movie star Pat O'Brien. A huge stage was built at Kingman Field for the extravaganza depicting the history of Ottawa.

The Wenona Centennial followed on July 28 - Aug. 2. The Coronation Ball featured the crowning of Miss Joan Kemp as the centennial queen in the high school gym. Mayor Ralph Goodwin gave her the key to the city and proclaimed her honorary city mayor for the week. Kemp's attendants included Bernadine Ricca, Margaret Nolan, Diane Kane, and Janet Tomlinson. On July 29, a crowd of 4,000 spectators packed the open-air theater to see "The Passing Years," a pageant of the city's history. Activities also included tours at the Swanson Cookie Factory and the Wenona Wear clothing factory. The high school gym was the scene of a square dance on July 30. At least 125 children participated in the Napper Day parade. The Wenona Index conservatively estimated 75,000 people took part in the centennial festivities.

Mendota's centennial celebration was held Aug. 9-15. Two thousand spectators lined the route from the fair grounds and back to watch the two-hour parade featuring 17 bands, 40 floats, and the cars carrying the Sweet Corn queen candidates. In the evening at the Sweet Corn Bowl, 4,000 spectators watched Carol Loach, the 1952 queen, crown the new queen Debby Heltness, a 17-year old Mendota H.S. senior.

Each day had a specific theme: Tot's and Teens Day, Sweet Corn Day, Fireworks Day, 100th Birthday, Fun Day, and Old Time Events Day. Among the festivities were two balloon ascensions. The first balloon would rise on Tuesday morning at Lake Mendota to highlight Sweet Corn Day. The second balloon went up on Thursday afternoon for the official 100th birthday party at which there was free cake for everyone.

Tonica also celebrated its centennial. The highlight came on Sept. 11 with a pageant at the grade school. A cast of 150 local citizens participated in the 15 historical scenes.

GAMBLING PROBLEMS PERSIST

There were still sporadic instances in 1953 when gambling in Bureau and LaSalle counties seemed to make a comeback. Harland Warren wasn't satisfied with putting only Tom Cawley out of business, there were others violating the law. The Becker-Currie cigar store in Peru was raided on May 2, 1953. Hoping to delay any surprise raids, Hugh (Red) Currie and Wilmer Becker, the owners of the cigar store, had partitioned off the poolroom in front from the back room where gambling was available. A heavy-duty, electrically-operated lock normally would have blocked entry to the back room, but on the day of the raid, the door was ajar.

During the raid, Currie signed a waiver so there was no need to secure a search warrant. Deputies Stanley Murray and James Cullens went in and found 13 pads of baseball tickets, 4 lucky jars with trade tickets, a bowl of ticket tape and $820 in cash. Becker and Currie posted bonds pending their trial.

Trying a new legal approach to discourage gamblers, the police prevented the 25 patrons from leaving until all their names were recorded. A little-used Peru ordinance made it a crime to patronize a gambling establishment.

Bureau County had also been active with gambling. In April 1953, the James Baracani tavern in Spring Valley was searched for gambling equipment. A complaint had been filed by John Colby of Hennepin, but when the case went before Justice Levering in Princeton, Colby refused to press charges. The judge fined Baracani $100 on a disorderly conduct charge and reminded him if there was a second gambling offense the penalty could be a $2,000 fine and a jail sentence.

Although gambling raids became less frequent, the state's attorneys continued in their futile attempts to eradicate gambling from the Illinois Valley. On Aug. 22, Warren ordered a raid in Streator at the Eagles Lodge. He knew the lodge had purchased a federal tax stamp and quickly proceeded to the location with Deputy Sheriff James Cullen, Streator Police Chief John Gaydos and Streator Mayor Albert Dietman. After finding a 25¢ slot machine, the mayor confiscated the tax stamp and revoked the lodge's city liquor license.

That same day in Princeton, Judge Hobart Gunning sentenced Harry J. Cassiday to pay $500 and court costs for possession of gambling equipment at the Cassiday billiard parlor in Spring Valley. At the sentencing, Gunning reminded the defendant, "Everyone in Bureau County knows how I feel about commercialized gambling…it should be stamped out."

Somebody didn't get that message or simply ignored it. On Nov. 20, 1953 at 10 p.m., 17 state police officers raided the Cassiday poolroom in Spring Valley and found enough gambling equipment - mostly punch boards lucky jars, football parley's and baseball tickets - to fill three trucks. After one truck was loaded with evidence, Harry A. Cassiday, the owner, allowed the officers to search the wholesale house next door. The total value of the confiscated materials was estimated at $24,000. Tom Cassiday and two employees, Ed Burke and Francis Sever, were arrested. The activity caused quite a commotion. About a hundred bystanders gathered to watch the state police load trucks and haul the material back to Princeton.

1954
FROM KOREA TO VIETNAM

Operation Big Switch, the exchange of POWs in Korea, was not without controversy. Especially troublesome was the refusal of a group of 21 Americans to be repatriated. Howard McGee, one of the speakers at the Hotel Kaskaskia, on Jan. 14 spoke about his experience in Korea and China with regard to the POWs. As a member of the UN team visiting the POWs he said he could not reveal the names of the men or give any information that might prevent any of them from returning to the US. His attempts to talk to the men privately were frustrated by the Communists. Traveling in Russian jeeps, which had dashboards that reminded him of a 1921 Ford, they were escorted with a Communist interpreter and a guard. He traveled across the Yalu River to visit the POWs and was followed by guards everywhere. Although a great deal of effort was made to convince the men to return to America, they persisted in their desire to stay in the communist world.

Some of the servicemen from the Illinois Valley continued to be recognized for their service in Korea. First Lt. Walter Mecozzi of Hennepin, was awarded a seventh oak leaf cluster for his Air Medal. The L-P Class of '42 graduate was a navigator on a B-26 attack bomber, which flew sustained operations in Korea. On one of his 50 missions, Mecozzi led a flight of six bombers in a daylight attack against the Communist offensive in May 1953.

Lt. Mecozzi flew in a B-26 similar to this one flying a mission over Korea.
USAF photo.

In March, M/Sgt. John A. Weberski from LaSalle, was awarded another Bronze Star for meritorious service in Korea. This was his fourth such award. According to a News-Tribune account, Weberski "served on Heartbreak Ridge and in the Kumwha Valley and guarded Communist prisoners on Koje-Do island." He was released from his active service duties in September 1953.

Another recipient of the Bronze Star was Cpl. Raymond Stachowiak of LaSalle. The machine gunner had distinguished himself for meritorious achievement by volunteering for numerous patrols since June 1953.

As citizens finally felt a return to normalcy with the end of fighting in Korea, there were ominous events in the Far East. The Viet Minh were attacking the French troops at Dien Bien Phu in northern Vietnam. It seemed to be a French problem, but the US was slowly becoming more involved by supplying C-47s to carry supplies to the French soldiers in the besieged outpost and, within a few months, the U.S. was providing planes to drop French paratroopers as reinforcements.

SAND BLOCKS THE TRACKS

Spring weather dominated the March news for towns along the Illinois River. A 7.5-inch snowfall blanketed the area at the beginning of March, setting a record for the heaviest snowfall in a decade. A few weeks later on Mar. 24, 4.09 inches of rain drenched the area. It was the heaviest 24-hour rainfall since the record-setting deluge of Oct. 11, 1931, when 4.57 inches soaked the area. Rt. 6 west of Hollowayville was covered with two inches of water, and the ground was covered three inches deep with golf ball-sized hail. Roland Lamps of Peru told a News-Tribune reporter he was driving to Hollowayville at 9:30 p.m. "It looked to me like snow. It got to the point where you couldn't steer the car. It was like driving in loose sand. If I hadn't experienced it, I wouldn't have believed it."

Both road and rail conditions were terrible. Rt. 89 south of Cherry was flooded out, and traffic on the bottom road at Route 51 was limited to one lane. The Illinois River measured a nine-foot rise below the Starved Rock dam. More significant for rail service was the sand slide that halted Rock Island passenger trains. Both the east and westbound tracks were covered with over four feet of sand. Three feet of sand covered the IC switch spur. End loaders were brought to the scene to remove an estimated 400 cubic yards of sand. Train traffic was stopped at 12:30 a.m. The eastbound *Rocket* from Chicago finally arrived at 3:32 a.m. The westbound Rock Island train didn't get to the depot until 5:32 a.m.

The next day, the river measured five feet over the 18-foot flood stage at LaSalle, but the river had crested. Two days of heavy rains caused the river to rise 13 feet. The bottomlands were flooded. Fortunately, it was March, and the crops were not yet planted. The Starved Rock State Park parking lot at the lower level was under water; the concession stand was surrounded by water. A more significant problem was faced by the towboats. The river current was so swift that a tow being moved by the *W. W. Marting* and the *Glenn Traer* had to be split into two tows of four barges each. One string of barges was tied off four miles upstream while the *Marting* went back to pick up the other four barges. Many basements were flooded in the Tri-Cities. A retaining wall at the Star Union Brewery in Peru gave way from the pressure of the rain-soaked ground. In Oglesby, the IC spur leading out of the Lehigh Portland Cement Co. was washed out; there were wet engines and mud piles at both the Lehigh and Marquette quarries.

MORE GAMBLING RAIDS IN THE VALLEY

More than any other recurring story, the battle to eliminate all forms of gambling consistently made the front-pages in the Illinois Valley. In February, the report of registered gambling stamp buyers showed a dramatic decline. Only 44 of the $50 gambling revenue stamps were registered locally. That could be compared to the 440 stamps purchased in Cook County. In mid-January, two raids had been carried out in Spring Valley. Mike Hopkins was charged with having gambling devices even though no evidence of gambling was found when Police Chief Joe Verucchi checked the establishment. In Seatonville, Quinto Errio, the operator of the Hill Top Tavern, was arrested on a warrant served by Sheriff Duffield. Like Hopkins, he was charged with having lottery tickets. Both men posted a $400 bond while awaiting a trial.

On Feb. 12, a raid was conducted at the Cassiday poolroom. The jury trial resulted in a fine of $250. In Ottawa, Clyde Frazier, owner of Frazier's Tap, was accused of a payoff to a customer playing the pinball machine. A trial was set for March 1. The whole question of the legality of pinball machines was under consideration by the General Assembly. Was winning on a pinball machine a game of chance or skill?

Another significant raid was conducted in mid-April in Peru. Ten officers simultaneously raided Ed Cosgrove's Singapore Tap and Ludwig Vogrich's Green Front Tavern on Fifth St. Joseph Jasiek, operator of the Castle Park Tavern at 1705 Pulaski, was also targeted. Surprisingly, the raids at Sajnaj's and Yanka's yielded nothing.

After two weeks surveillance at Cassiday's, Sheriff Duffield conducted the most dramatic roundup of scofflaw violators in Spring Valley on April 23. At exactly 10 p.m., 30 raiders hit the Cassiday poolroom and local bars.

Cassiday pool hall in Spring Valley. Spring Valley library collection.

Twenty individuals, mostly bartenders, faced gambling charges. Harry Cassiday, who was charged on Nov. 20, 1953, was once again charged with operating a gaming house. He posted a $4,000 bond for himself and $400 bonds for three of his employees. The other locations of gambling equipment included Baracani's Bar, the Bee Hive Dairy Bar, the Cottage Junction, Sally's Tavern, Pep Frasco Tavern, Ray's Tavern, Andy's Tap, and the Texas Inn. Most were located on East St. Paul Street.

Most of the cases were heard on May 11. The defendants generally plead guilty and paid the fine and costs, usually amounting to about $300. The case against George and Joseph Nimee, owners of the Bee Hive Dairy Bar, was continued one week but essentially ended the same way. Since the Bee Hive was operated as a confectionary not a tavern, Judge Hobart Gunning felt it was "more vulnerable morally." If the brothers were found guilty of a second offense, he cited the penalty as $500 and six months in the county jail. For their first offense, they only received fines amounting to $150 and $300.

It was standing room only in the Bureau county jail in Princeton. The 20 defendants and 29 officers filled the booking area. The police worked until 5 a.m., taking inventory and filling two trucks with pinball machines, lucky jars, baseball tickets, punchboards, boxes of candy, and a baseball scoreboard. They also seized several thousand dollars in cash as evidence. Cassiday, who was not present during the raid, commented on the crackdown to a News-Tribune reporter, "The state doesn't want any open gambling so we put it behind closed doors. Then this happens."

Periodically, the police also raided the "houses of ill repute." In late April, LaSalle sheriff's deputies arrested five women working in two brothels. Mary Anderson, 60, was charged with operating the Gay Mill in Jonesville. Her two "inmates" from Chicago were also arrested. At the Elms, Maxinne Kerosoda, 62, was in charge of the house. A 24-year old girl from Chicago was charged as an "inmate." The "customers" all left hurriedly without being charged.

SUMMERTIME CELEBRATIONS

As in previous years, several towns were celebrating their centennials. The Burlington and Missouri River RR engine No. 35, built in 1881 and mail car No. 1 was scheduled to arrive for the Buda festivities on July 3-5.

The Burlington No. 35 engine and mail car photo appeared in the July 1, 1954 edition of the News-Tribune.

Entertainment during the spring and summer of 1954 brought some of the best orchestras to the area.

Louis Armstrong was much in demand. He only played in Chicago and Spring Valley that year.

In June, Johnnie Kaye was ready with some great rhythms at Indian Acres in Streator.

Les Brown's outstanding band was coming in August. The Crew Cuts would perform their latest hit, "Sh-Boom," with the Teddy Phillips Orchestra at the Spring Valley ballroom in September.

A crowd estimated at 50,000 attended the Kewanee Centennial later in July. Amboy's 100th birthday was held Aug. 6-8. Children in Amboy participated in their own parade on Saturday. Governor Stratton was one of the guests of honor in the two-mile Grand Parade on Aug. 8.

Mendota held its 7th annual Sweet Corn Festival on Aug. 9-10. Sue Rave was crowned queen by Debby Heltness in the high school auditorium. A crowd of 25,000 watched one hundred floats in the Mendota parade. Donald Kettleborough, 9, riding in a miniature car, won a first prize. After the parade, tons of buttered corn were served at the IC freight depot.

Although none of the towns in Putnam County were celebrating anniversaries, there were the usual homecomings. The weekend of Aug 13-15 was especially busy with festivities in Hennepin and Mark. On Aug. 14, Hennepin held a children's parade on the waterfront. The adult participants were led by Amos "Bud" Deininger riding on his stallion while carrying the American flag. Mayor Frank Biagi, Fire Chief Marion Kuhne, and Ben Cassell, commander of the American Legion post. followed in a car. Prizes were awarded to Patricia Bouxsein, Patricia Grasser, Emma Ellena, Gerald and Larry Kline, Gerald Grasser, Mary Jo Bassi, Janice Eattoni, and Janice Walters. A street dance completed the Saturday events. On Sunday, the Regatta boat races and water show attracted a large crowd.

That same weekend, the Mark Fire Department sponsored the village's 4th Homecoming. Food tents, rides, and concession stands filled the area next to the old coal dump. The Great Eugene High Wire Act amazed the crowd. Reflecting its Italian heritage, the homecoming would not have been complete without a boccie ball tournament and ravioli and spaghetti dinners. The Spring Valley Italian-American Clown Band added to the ethnic entertainment. News- Tribune ad.

One of the last major summertime celebrations involved the opening of the new Rt. 51 highway (Rt. 351 today) from Shippingsport Bridge to LaSalle in August. Although an approach road was built in 1913, it was subject to frequent flooding.

Festivities began on Saturday, Aug 28, 1954, with children's pet parade, carnival rides, and a hot-air balloon ascension. A crowd, estimated at 10,000, gathered at Second and Tonti to watch Matt Sebastian parachute from the balloon at 600 feet. The Spring Valley Municipal Band performed in the evening.

On Sunday, there were concerts by the Peru and Oglesby city bands. The thousands who came for the ribbon-cutting ceremony by Gov. William Stratton stood in the hot afternoon sun during the speeches by the state and city officials. In case of any medical emergencies, Olin Gearhart, a LaSalle mortician, stood by with his ambulance.

After the dedication speeches, the governor cut the magenta ribbon. Hoping to be the first car to cross the new roadway, Al Brady of Spring Valley drove his car from the bridge to LaSalle. The police stopped him as he came up the Rt. 51 hill to get his name. In the process, he was passed by another car driven by G. E. Hassler of rural Princeton, who technically was the first to cross into LaSalle. Bill Vogel of LaSalle drove the first car heading south to Oglesby.

There were many other activities on Sunday. An aerial platform was erected for acrobatic feats. In the evening, Joe DiZutti's orchestra played for a street dance.

WESTCLOX BATTLES THE SWISS

It's not often that a local problem requires congressional action, but in the summer of '54 Westclox executives went to the nation's capital to plead their case against Swiss watch and clock manufacturers. George H. Smith, assistant superintendent, and W. B. Sampson, both residents of Peru, testified before a Senate Preparedness Subcommittee about the unfair trade practices of the Swiss. It was not the first time that American clock manufacturers had to defend their industry. The Senators had heard previous testimony about the essential aspect of the Westclox defense contributions in WWII. The Swiss had taken over the domestic market while Westclox was supplying the military with bomb fuses. Company executives argued for protection to insure a place in the domestic market during peacetime. They felt there would not be enough jobs for domestic production due to cheap Swiss imports, and a valuable labor force would be lost.

The Congress responded by recommending an increase in the tariff to a maximum 50 percent increase on Swiss watch movements of less than 17 jewels. This would raise the duty to as much as $2.50 on each movement. President Eisenhower agreed and said the higher tariff was necessary to avoid injury to an industry, which had to be preserved for "national defense." As expected, the Swiss government lodged protests against the new tariff rates. Westclox vice president and general manager A.J. Hasselman praised Eisenhower's decision. Other industrial leaders joined in their approval of Eisenhower's decision to raise the rate.

THE GREAT FLOOD OF '54

Usually, it was during the spring rains that residents along the Illinois River anticipated a rising river with the possibility of flooding. However, a 2.6-inch rainfall in October produced a record-setting flood. All of the gates were opened at the Starved Rock Dam, but so great was the flow that the lower pool below the dam rose to within a foot of the water in the upper pool. Ottawa H.S. and Marquette H.S. football fields were under water as were many of the low-lying farm fields. The Fox River carried away partially sunken boats.

Many agencies responded to the emergency. The Army Corps of Engineers was ready to secure barges that had broken away from moorings near Peru, but the area engineer was limited by the skeleton crew at his disposal. Gov. William Stratton sent the National Guard to Ottawa at the request of Ottawa Mayor Philip Bailey. Coast Guard units were also sent to Ottawa on Oct. 11. The Red Cross was busy providing shelter for homeless families in Dayton, Sheridan, and Wedron. Water three to five feet deep poured over the Dayton Dam. "The river is the highest I've ever seen it in my 35 years here," said Supt. John Dummett of Wedron Silica. Long time residents of Earlville made similar remarks about Indian Creek. The blacktop connecting Earlville and Rollo was impassable.

The floodwaters subsided almost as quickly as they rose. The Coast Guard and National Guard units were released, but the Red Cross volunteers still manned their tent in Ottawa on East Superior St. and sent in a mobile unit to Wedron. Floodwaters continued to cover the lower areas of Starved Rock State Park.

1955
FIRES ACROSS THE ILLINOIS VALLEY

Nothing was more devastating to a small town than a major fire. On Jan. 31, 1955 at 12:30 a.m., three of Buda's largest downtown businesses went up in flames. Even with five fire departments responding, it appeared that the community of 750 would lose a historic building known as the Lockwood Block. It included four businesses: Stutzman's Hardware Store, the Fred Stratton and Son locker plant, the Warner Drug Store, and the Walter Whipple implement and appliance shop. The blaze appeared to have started in the locker plant.

Pictured is a portion of the burned-out remains of the Lockwood Block. The library and post office to the right sustained only water damage in the half million dollar fire.

News-Tribune photo.

The Buda fire station, located directly opposite of the inferno, quickly had its 35-man force on the job, but more help was needed. The Wyanet, Manlius, Sheffield, and Bradford fire departments responded. Ninety men battled the flames in near-zero weather until 5:30 a.m. when the fire was brought under control. The firemen kept their hoses on the adjoining buildings, the Martin barbershop, the apartments housing Mrs. Haley and the Lang family, the library, the post office, and a grocery store.

Reflecting on the damage, Fred Stratton sadly recalled that the building was one of Buda's landmarks. Built in 1870 by a blind Civil War veteran, the building once housed the Masonic temple and opera house. The entertainment center once drew the best road shows, presenting such epics as "Uncle Tom's Cabin." A Swiss bell ringers group also played at the opera house. Fire Chief A.G. (Barney) Stinson estimated the damage at $500,000.

LaSalle's downtown was the scene of a major fire that broke out in the old Kelly-Cawley building in the 600 block of First Street on Feb. 20. Smoke was first detected at the rear of the Cawley building at 4:30 a.m. A short time later, clouds of smoke were pouring from the former dining room of the casino.

Because of the intense heat, cracks developed in the brickwork.
Officials feared the large Kelly-Cawley sign was in danger of falling on pedestrians.
Ryan Cawley collection.

By 7 a.m., Frank Groleski's shoe store was completely engulfed; the fire quickly spread to the second floor. Adjoining shops were generally vacant. However, Field's apparel shop suffered significant water and smoke damage as two LaSalle fire companies and the Peru fire department poured water on the blaze for several hours. By 9 a.m., the fire had broken through the roof and had spread through the old tavern. Two hours later, the roof began to collapse.

Cawley had arranged to have his casino on the 600 block of LaSalle torn down. Since most of the structure had been vacant since 1953, it was insured for only $20,000 – far less than its estimated value of $200,000. A modern J.C. Penney building would soon replace the old casino. Photo from Oglesby library collection.

The next significant fire occurred on April 27 in downtown Henry. The source of the fire that began at 1:15 a.m. was thought to be an abandoned icehouse. In addition to the Henry fire department, other units responded from Lacon, Princeton, and Chillicothe. When the flames crossed Rt. 18 to the Watercott building, the LaSalle and Peoria departments were alerted. The Mallard Motor Co. lost several vehicles and boats as well as automotive equipment. One of the vehicles was a fully loaded Prairie Farm ice cream truck. The Lucas garage building suffered extensive damage. Wiedman's variety store and the icehouse were completely destroyed.

On May 27, a lightning strike at 12:35 a.m. started a $75,000 fire in Spring Valley's Hunter-Doherty lumberyard. The flames shot 300 feet into the air. The heavy downpour during the storm helped the firemen from Spring Valley, Ladd, and Peru to contain the blaze. The 120-foot shed that was struck was fully loaded with lumber, causing the flames to spread quickly. The power tools in the shed were destroyed.

Two other smaller sheds containing sheet metal and gutters burned to the ground. The contents of a third shed were wrecked by water damage. Fortunately, Spring Valley Mayor William Savitch, one of the business partners, and Frank Stuart, a company driver, were able to move seven trucks housed in the buildings to a safe location.

About four months later, Spring Valley suffered another major fire. On Sunday afternoon, Oct. 2, Peter Hollerich, a cashier at the Spring Valley City Bank, smelled smoke coming from the Steinberg department store. He immediately notified the fire department and Maurice Steinberg, one of the owners. In addition to five trucks of the Spring Valley fire department, units from Ladd and Peru also responded. Although the two-story building was destroyed, the Steinberg warehouse and the bank on either side of the store were saved during the nine-hour fire. After the fire, Harry Steinberg said he would rebuild on the same site.

Peru firemen were called out again on Oct. 5 to battle a fire at the Comparon Motor company located west of Peru. "Red" Wasik spotted the fire at 4:30 a.m. while driving his bread delivery truck. He called Walter Ratajczak, the motor company manager, who in turn called in the alarm. The Peru fire department was aided with the arrival of a water tanker from William Sale and Sons. The flames were put out quickly so there was no damage to the cars located on the main floor.

On Nov. 29, an early morning fire destroyed almost one-third of the business district in Rutland. The six-hour fire was too big for the Rutland and Minonk volunteer fire departments. Walls came crashing down three times as the men fought both the flames and the 14^0 temperature, which left a coating of ice on the streets and sidewalks. The effort to save the buildings was given up at 9:30 a.m. although the fire continued until 10 a.m. The post office building owned by Mr. and Mrs. Sheldon Roland, Leila Bane's grocery, Steve Francisco's tavern, and the Masonic hall were destroyed in the $100,000 fire.

THE LAST ILLINOIS CENTRAL STEAM ENGINE

The transition to all diesel engines for the Illinois Central became apparent in LaSalle at the beginning of 1955. The diesel-powered engines already replaced the old steam engines for on the Rock Island and Burlington trains coming through the Tri-Cities. Illinois Central engine No. 2122 was the last functioning steam engine to leave LaSalle. Train 397 headed south over the mile-long bridge to Oglesby, and from there, it would head to Clinton to be scrapped. Attached to the train were two other partially dismantled steam engines. Another steam engine remained in the LaSalle yards while its pistons were removed. Once that was accomplished, the engine was also scheduled to be dead-headed to Clinton. The local trains from LaSalle that traveled to Freeport and Clinton were discontinued. The age of steam and black smoke was ending.

Two ICRR men from Amboy, E.C. Lane, conductor, and Charles Mickey, engineer wearing a white cap, took Engine No. 2122, out of LaSalle on Jan. 17, 1955. It was headed on its final run to Clinton, IA. Standing next to the train are V.C. Shelley, trainmaster, and William Confrey, general agent. Photo by Bob Johns.

The Rock Island's diesel-powered *Rockets* seemed to be a wave of future until the mid-50's. In June of 1954, the Rock Island had ordered a new passenger train consisting of a new light-weight engine and four cars. It was hoped the new trains, dubbed the *Jet Rockets,* would make the trip between Peoria and Chicago in little more than two hours. The cars, sheeted in stainless steel, were due to be introduced in December 1955.

A SLOW DEATH FOR GAMBLING

"Little Reno" was never quite the same for those who enjoyed the food, gambling, and entertainment in the clubs run by Tinney Cosgrove and Tom Cawley. However, some taverns still made a few dollars on low-keyed gambling in the form of lucky jars, lottery tickets, and punch boards. On Feb. 12, 1955, Mayor Bruno accompanied the police in raids at four locations At the United Cigar Store at 541 First St. they found a Santa Anita sweepstakes book on the counter as well as a collegiate basketball schedule and a sports wire. Two jars of "lucky" tickets were found at El Mirador. Weller's Tavern at 1058 Eighth St. also had tickets, basketball parley cards, and sweepstake tickets. The fourth place raided, Clem's tavern, had no illegal materials. The three owners, Fred Duffy (United Cigar Store), Sam Weingard (El Mirador), and George Welter (Welter's Tavern) were each fined $100.

Another raid the next day resulted in only two arrests out of the twelve locations investigated. The two owners caught with gambling paraphernalia were William Baima (329 Third St.) and John Dinotto (101 Second St. – the former Starlight Inn). They received $50 fines. There just didn't seem to be as much interest in the old games. The "lucky" jars were covered with dust in both of the taverns. Nobody had tried their luck in many months.

The fines had little impact on the behavior of the tavern owners. Cassiday's poolroom was targeted on April 25. Bureau county deputies confiscated tip boards, dice, and $750 in a cigar box along with baseball pool tickets and 50 cents worth of metal tokens. Dominic Chiodo was arrested but freed on a $2,000 bond. Harry A. Cassiday, the owner, was not on the premises but had court date in October at the Hennepin courthouse on charges of possession of gambling devices.

Gambling raids continued into the fall with an Aug. 14 raid on the Ki and Johns Tavern. Police confiscated some baseball cards and a few 8 and 11 boards. John Witek, the bartender was arrested. He admitted he was selling the 25¢ tickets off and on for six months.

At the end of September, sheriff's deputies made a more significant haul at Eddie Bulak's tavern in DePue. Two craps tables, two lucky jars, nine punchboards, a bag of Big Charley tickets, four boxes of poker chips, and a gambling clock were taken to the Princeton jail. When his case came up on the court docket, Bulak's admission of guilt resulted in a swift fine of $100.

Bulak had even a bigger problem since he and Harry Cassiday were facing a trial in Hennepin for trying to bribe a Bureau county deputy. Eventually, they were both fined $3,000 for attempted bribery.

Another raid in late September took place at the Eclipse poolroom in Spring Valley. It was a similar story; the police confiscated football pools, lottery tickets, punch boards, and a tip board. Bernard Ballerine, one of the owners was taken to the courthouse in Princeton and posted bond.

On Oct. 24, Harry A. Cassiday had his day in the Hennepin courtroom. After the closing arguments, the jury took only five minutes to find him guilty of the charges leveled against him for the Nov. 20, 1953 raid on his warehouse, possession of gambling equipment. His defense that he had transferred ownership to his son, Jack Cassiday, and his son-in-law, John Cosgrove, did not affect the decision. The prosecutor made his case by pointing out that Harry Cassiday had a key to the warehouse and that meant he had possession. Judge Albert Pucci fined Cassiday $500. His defense attorney immediately appealed the ruling.

Bureau County seemed to be one of the areas where gambling lingered. On Nov. 28, state police raided the Rocket Café and Tap in Bureau and Andy's Tap in Spring Valley. Ray Howland, the proprietor at the Bureau tavern, was charged with having a pinball machine, a jar of tickets and a package of dice.

At the Spring Valley bar, the police only confiscated a pinball machine. There was quite a bit of controversy over pinball machines as games of chance or skill, but under the law, states attorneys tended to view them as gambling devices. Andrew Taliani, owner of Andy's Tap at 100 E. Dakota, was not immediately apprehended.

REMINDERS OF A BYGONE ERA

Cedar Point, long known for its coal mining operation that began with the sinking of a shaft in 1904, was in the news in April due to a fear that a serious cave-in might occur on the Basilio Capitani farm. Although the 533-foot mineshaft had been sealed in 1922, the area around the entrance was beginning to deteriorate. In April 1955, it was decided to fill the shaft since the bottom had 350 feet of water. The cost would be shared by Capitani and the Union Coal Co., which purchased all mineral rights from the LaSalle Carbon Coal Co.

Another reminder of the coal-mining era came later in the year with the death of Frank Zanarini, 69, at St., Margaret's Hospital on Aug. 13. He was the last survivor among the 21 miners who were rescued after being trapped underground for over a week during the Cherry mine fire of 1909.

WAGING WAR ON POLIO

After years of research and testing, the Salk polio vaccine was ready for inoculations of first and second graders in the Tri-Cities. The first news came on April 16, but it would still be a few weeks before the first free shots would be given. Second and third shot were recommend by Dr. Salk. John McCann, the LaSalle county chairman of the Foundation for Infantile Paralysis, picked up the vaccine in Chicago on April 18. The supply for Bureau, Marshall, and Lee counties was distributed through Springfield.

First and second graders from Wenona and Varna received shots on April 21. The inoculations began in Spring Valley the same day at the Lincoln School where a medical center was set up. It only took 40 minutes to vaccinate 160 children. A second inoculation clinic was planned for May 12. The youngsters were bussed from Ladd, Arlington, Cherry,

Hollowayville, Seatonville, and Dalzell. Children from the Grant School and Immaculate Conception School walked to the Lincoln School. Dr. Silvio Davito and Dr. T.C. Ahnger of Spring Valley and Dr. A Cardenes of Ladd supervised the program along with six nurses. The school superintendents and a number of volunteers assisted in processing paperwork and other duties. On April 25, Jean Panneck, 7, a second grader at St. Mary's in Peru, was the first pupil to receive the polio vaccine in the Tri-Cities. Because of safety concerns with the new vaccine, the second series of shots was delayed until November. In the battle against polio, not everyone was protected. By November, 21 cases were reported in LaSalle County. It would take decades to eradicate it.

COLD WAR FEARS PERSIST

Preparation for a war with the Soviet Union was waged as vigorously as the war on polio. From February through May 1955, Operation Teapot, a series of 14 nuclear tests, were conducted in Nevada. On May 5, the men in a tank unit, designated Task Force Razor, were positioned only a few thousand meters from the detonation tower. One of those to take part in the Apple-2 test was Pfc. George W. Washer of rural Zearing. The gunner with the 723rd Tank Battalion was one of 800 men in the tank unit deployed to assess the impact. Patton tanks were positioned 50 yards apart and about 3,000 yards from ground zero. Further back were M59 armored personnel carriers. The tank commander later said, "I believe we could move them in to 2,000 yards, and some of our people say 1,500."

In the Apple-2 test on May 5, 1955, both civilians and military personnel watched the 29-kiloton nuclear detonation.
DoD photo.

Mannequins were used to simulate the effects on civilians involved in various activities in "Survival Town" when the blast occurred.

The Apple-2 test was filmed for the documentary "Operation Cue." In 1983, producers of a TV movie, "The Day After," used film segments of the Nevada test to dramatize the effects of an atomic blast on buildings. DoD photos.

During the summer of 1955, a nationwide test of nuclear war preparedness was conducted. The exercise in Illinois involved a simulated nuclear attack on Chicago and St. Louis. Civil defense units would take part in a nine-day response scenario compressed into 26-hours.

The Tri-Cities units were involved based on the premise that if the Chicago area was bombed, the radioactive fallout would reach the area within four hours. If a real attack took place, the LaSalle squadron of the Civil Air Patrol was responsible for collecting radioactive fallout in the clouds to determine the intensity and wind direction to plan when the fallout would reach the Tri-Cities.

Although the exercise predicted fallout would reach as far as Peoria, not everyone was a willing participant. Marvin Merritt, civil defense director in Peoria, complained the repeated tests would cause a loss of pay for thousands of volunteers. Except for Merritt's staff and a few key volunteers, Peoria was not going to cooperate. The lack of participation in Peoria did not create a major problem. It was still possible to assess the casualties to 61 major cities and industrial areas and 600 other likely targets. Operation Alert was an eye-opener for President Eisenhower who said, "The disaster produced more complications than I ever believed possible."

Operation Skywatch had few local participants in June. Unorganized GOC posts were located in Leonore, Granville, and Magnolia. Ken Nunn, the Illinois Central station agent, was the lone spotter for the Oglesby GOC. He was responsible for reporting to the filter center any unidentified planes, but he only manned the post during daylight hours. Ed Rashid ran the observation post in Streator. Three other posts were located in Grand Ridge, Kernan, and Garfield. There would be few observers available for the "Look to the Sky in July" Skywatch program unless more volunteers stepped forward.

SUMMERTIME IN THE VALLEY

Although the Rose Bowl tavern, the last of the popular nightspots on LaSalle's "gay white way" closed in late May, there were many activities to keep civilian minds off the threat of nuclear war. Ladd was playing host to the 16th District American Legion Convention in early July. A carnival-like atmosphere was planned for July 2 complete with a pet parade, water fights, a baseball game, and singing and dancing. The following day was set aside for church services, convention business, a parade of American Legion units, and an exhibition by the drum and bugle corps of the Black Knights of Kewanee.

Mark was celebrating its golden jubilee and fifth Homecoming that same weekend. On July 1, an evening fish fry was followed by a street dance. The program on Saturday called for another dance. A bocci ball tournament and more musical entertainment were scheduled for Sunday. The final events included a parade of 51 units, musical entertainment, and a fireworks finale. The guest of honor was Mark Elliott, son of the town's founder, John Elliott.

Princeton was celebrating "Q-Days" July 28-30. Residents were encouraged to come down to the depot to see the old No. 85 Burlington engine and mail car.

For those interested in the prehistoric history of the area, the Illinois Valley Expedition during the summer of '55 offered a glimpse into the lives of the Hopewell Indians. The Adolph Kuhne farm, located in Putnam County about five miles north of Henry, was the scene of an archaeological dig directed by Dr. Stuart Struever of Peru. The excavation of the village was a first in that the participants were mainly untrained high school students from the area. Carla Saari, Peter Schultz, James Ponti, and Richard Devecchio were selected from the applicants at L-P H.S. The students from Hall H.S. working on the dig were Patricia Podobinski, Sally Norris, Allen Overton, and Marion Kujawa. Walter Sarbaugh was selected as a sole representative of Magnolia-Swaney H.S. in McNabb. Two college students rounded out the excavation team. Thousands of artifacts were unearthed during the summer-long dig. [Note: Over 100 students from Putnam County H.S. in the author's archaeology classes conducted excavations at the same location during the 1980's. The artifacts discovered at that time are currently used in the author's American history classes at IVCC.]

For the younger generation a new fad was sweeping the country. Superman and Hopalong Cassidy were being replaced by another American hero. A revival of interest in the legendary Davy Crockett was inspired by the release of Walt Disney's motion picture "Davy Crockett-King of the Wild Frontier." LaSalle mayor B.D. Bruno brought attention to the symbol of American frontier folklore with a Davy

Crockett Days proclamation. He urged youngsters to commemorate Crockett's deeds during Aug. 11-13. The management at the Majestic Theater offered prizes for the youngsters wearing the best Davy Crockett costumes at the performances.

A more somber observance of American history took place in Oglesby on Aug. 13-14. The Thomas Larkin American Legion Post 237 organized a parade and memorial service to observe the tenth anniversary of V-J Day. American flags lined Walnut St. during the two-day observance. On Sunday, post commander Ray Baysour unveiled the monument dedicated to those who served in WWII and Korea and those who gave their lives for their country. Rev. C.A. Mayes, pastor of the Holy Family Church, gave the dedication address.

For only $2.50 music lovers had the opportunity to listen to Lawrence Welk and his 24-piece orchestra on Sept. 13. Buzz Verucchi booked the show for one of the two nights when they were playing in Illinois.

On Sept. 15, a different form of entertainment was coming to Peru and Spring Valley. The arrival of the stern-wheeler *Avalon* was a rare occurrence since the boat generally cruised the Ohio and Mississippi rivers. The ship was built in Pittsburg in 1914 and was originally used as a ferryboat. In 1930, it was converted to an excursion boat. The four-deck steamer had plenty of room with a capacity of 1,370 passengers and a crew of 42.

A crowd of 761 young people boarded the old stern-wheeler for an afternoon excursion. Three priests from St. Bede, the Rev. Bernard Horzen, the Rev. Dunston Morrissey, and the Rev. Alfred Schiedler supervised the 94 students from the academy. There were also three Benedictine nuns on board to supervise the seventh and eight graders from St. Roch's School in LaSalle. For many of the youngsters, it was their first ride on a steamboat. As the boat pulled away from the Peru dock, Captain Ernest Wagner rang the departure bell.

In the evening, hundreds of adults took the moonlight cruise down the Illinois River and listened to the Rhythm Masters, a 9-piece band. Some of the passengers remembered excursions in bygone years. As the band played, some passengers were attracted to the half dozen motor boats that were escorting the big steamer on its 16-mile round trip. As the *Avalon* returned to the dock, the captain blew the ship's horn to announce its arrival. After this excursion, the captain took the *Avalon* downriver to Peoria for a three-day weekend excursion.

Originally christened the *Idlewild,* the steamer cruised up the Illinois River during the Great Depression and WWII for excursions at LaSalle-Peru-Spring Valley. After WWII, the *Idlewild* was sold to J. Herold Gorsage of Peoria in 1948 and rechristened the *Avalon.* In 1962, the city of Louisville purchased the boat and rechristened it the *Belle of Louisville.* The ship had a full sailing schedule for 2010!

A ROCK ISLAND RR INNOVATION

The 1950's was a period of continued expansion of the Rock Island *Rocket* passenger trains, but there were unfortunate setbacks for the railroad overall. The switchmen's strike in 1950 brought the Rock Island to a standstill. It was the first time in 98 years that the entire line was stopped. Within two weeks, the trains were moving again, but the loss of revenue coupled with a costly wage increase was crippling.

Something new was needed to increase passenger traffic. The task fell to the Electro-Motive division of General Motors. Their engineers designed the "Y" train, a lightweight power car with a 1,200-hp engine combined with coaches that could carry 400 passengers at 100 mph.

The *Jet Rocket* made a test run from Chicago to Seneca on Aug. 22, 1955. The trip took only 62 minutes. Author's collection.

On the initial run to the Illinois Valley, the *Jet Rocket* rounded the most dangerous curves at an average speed of 82 mph. The new train, carrying 55 passengers, hit a top speed of 103 mph and broke all Rock Island speed records. Included among the passengers on the historic trip were Rock Island executives and design engineers. After the initial inspection, the engineer backed the *Jet Rocket* onto the "Y" of the old Seneca and Kankakee RR and reversed directions to head back. Although the model used on Aug. 22 was a "demonstrator," the public was assured when service began between Chicago and Peoria, the trains would be virtually identical.

THE MURDER OF TRADER JACK

Murders in the Illinois Valley were rare, but one in particular stood out in the 1950's. One of the most notable figures in the history of Granville was John S. Redshaw. Known as "Trader Jack" for his wheeling and dealing business acumen, some of his activities resulted in dangerous and potentially deadly confrontations with criminal elements.

Jack Redshaw's warehouse in Granville housed thousands of items.

This interior view of the Redshaw warehouse shows the vast variety of goods he traded. Photos contributed by John L. Redshaw.

Redshaw guards the valuables in the old Granville State Bank vault. Photo contributed by John L. Redshaw.

One incident occurred on Jan. 22, 1931, when a potential customer lured Redshaw to his downtown office in the old Granville State Bank building. Arriving at his office, four men holding pistols and a sawed-off shotgun confronted Redshaw. They pulled a $1,000 diamond ring from his hand and took the money from his wallet. Then they demanded that he open his vault, which usually contained valuable gems. Redshaw pleaded poverty due to a previous robbery, and his abductors believed him. Instead, the would-be robbers hustled him into a waiting car and drove off, followed by two more men in another car. One gunman continued to jab Redshaw in the chest with the shotgun as they fled south. Traveling about three miles, they stopped the car and told Redshaw to get out. One man apparently thought he would at least take Jack's large raccoon coat as a trophy of their theft. He shouted, "All right, shed the coat buddy," After handing over the coat, Redshaw walked about 200 yards before one of the robbers shouted, "Hey Redshaw, come back and get your coat." Jack was a very large man, and the coat was much too big for the muggers, who fled after giving back his coat. Redshaw hurried into town and contacted the police, who issued an all-points bulletin. No one was apprehended, but the police speculated that the crime might have involved members of "Egan's Rats," a notorious gang based in St. Louis, MO. State's Attorney Durley Boyle said Redshaw later told him he "would not be taken for a ride again." "I doubt he would have opened the safe knowing he would have been killed whether he would have opened it or not," Boyle told a reporter.

Another attempt to break into the Redshaw vault occurred on Jan. 1, 1953. Trader Jack was not on the premises when burglars forced open a rear door to gain access to the old bank vault. The bandits wore gloves to avoid leaving fingerprints and secured rugs to the top of the vault with tape to prevent any passerby from seeing their activity around the vault door. They used an acetylene torch to drill two holes into the 1½-ton steel door but were still unable to open the vault. The damage to the vault door can still be seen. Photo by author.

At 8 a.m. the next morning, Jack unlocked the door to his office. Although the vault was not opened, he found a number of items were missing. The burglars grabbed a pair of binoculars, a few personal items, and two pearl-handled pistols, a .45 and a gold-plated .38. Redshaw reported the break-in to the authorities. Putnam County Sheriff James A.

Hynds and LaSalle County Deputy Sheriff Dave Monterastelli dusted for fingerprints as part of their investigation, but nothing further developed from the investigation. One witness saw three men driving away in a dark colored Olds 88 parked across the street. According to the News-Tribune, Redshaw had a "vast collection of gems, paintings, guns, and bric-a-brac, including such items as $150,000 worth of diamonds on a single tray, a star ruby of 102 carats and chest upon chest of emeralds, opals, sapphires, amethysts, and other gems."

Trader Jack is pictured showing a piece of jewelry to a customer. John L. Redshaw collection.

The dealings of Redshaw were well known, and perhaps because of his notoriety as an international trader, he was murdered on Sept. 27, 1955. The WWI veteran and former Granville postmaster was found by his wife, Mary, a few minutes before noon on that fateful day.

Jeno Bonucchi was the owner of the Royal Blue grocery store, which was located a few buildings south of the murder scene. Recalling the incident in October 2009, he said Mary had called in an order to be delivered to her house at about 9:30 a.m. Busy at work, he was not able to deliver the order until an hour or so later. Had he not been delayed, he thought Mary might have also been a murder victim.

After Bonucchi dropped off the groceries at the Redshaw home, Mary left to join her husband for lunch after first stopping at the post office and the bank. When Mary arrived at her husband's office a little before noon, she knocked at the door, but there was no answer. She tried the door and found it to be ajar, an unusual situation because it was always kept locked even when her husband was inside. Suspicious that something was wrong, she went down the street to the Ellena hardware store and asked one of the boys to come down to the old bank building. He went in first and discovered her husband's body.

The old Granville State Bank on McCoy St. was the scene of the most famous murder mystery in the history of Granville. Mary continued to operate a business in the building. It was later converted into the town library and township office. Photo from John L. Redshaw collection.

Redshaw's body was found slumped in the narrow passageway in the vault. An unloaded sub-machinegun was at his side, but there was no immediate indication of foul play. A blood-stained figurine also laid beside the body. The object usually was located on a top shelf in the vault. At first, Mary thought it must have fallen and stuck her husband, since there was a gash on his head. Thinking he was only knocked unconscious from the blow, she took his wrist trying to feel a pulse. Finding none, she tried again touching the jugular vein. It was then that her finger touched a hole in his neck. At that point, according to Bill Tonarelli, she rushed down to his snack shop and yelled, "Bill, call the sheriff and call the doctor."

This Thompson sub-machinegun was found next to Redshaw's body. It is kept in the Putnam County courthouse. Photo by author.

Passing by across the street, Jane Germano was drawn to the commotion at the Redshaw building. She went inside and noticed the powder burns on the wound. This was no mere accident.

Still unsure if Redshaw was actually deceased, Deputy Coroner Robert L. Cofoid, Frank Laymon, Ed Vogel, and Bill Tonarelli lifted the 300-pound man into the Dysart ambulance, attempting to rush him to St. Margaret's Hospital. Tonarelli recalled in a 2009 interview how it was difficult to move the body over one of the counters in front of the vault. "Blood was dripping over everything," Tonarelli said. Seeing Dr. Birgerson entering his home two blocks away, they stopped immediately. The doctor pronounced Redshaw deceased.

Jack's body was taken to the Dysart Chapel where the coroner discovered three bullet holes in the corpse. One bullet entered the left side of the stomach. Another hole was found under the left arm, and a third bullet hole was the one originally discovered by Mary in her husband's throat.

That same afternoon, Coroner Howard Dysart impaneled a jury. Investigators were also summoned from the state crime laboratory. Hoping more information about the murder might be uncovered after the police investigation, the inquest was delayed until Thursday.

Redshaw's funeral was held on Thursday at the Dysart Chapel. The Granville American Legion gave their former post commander military honors at the Granville Cemetery.

Although he survived other attacks, unknown assailants murdered "Trader Jack" in his vault on Sept. 27, 1955. His body was found inside the vault. Photo by author.

One piece of evidence in the mystery was the discovery of an abandoned 1955 two-tone green Oldsmobile (similar to the sketch) found three miles west of Granville on Rt. 71.

Mrs. Vivian Anderson of Granville said she had seen the same or a very similar vehicle, occupied by two men wearing grey hats and cruising downtown Monday morning. Another report stated that an Olds was seen parked in front of the Redshaw building at 10:20 a.m. The Olds found on Rt. 71

was towed to the Granville Motor Co. Further investigation indicated the car was stolen as were the license plates, which were assigned to a Dodge registered in the Chicago area.

When the coroner's jury convened, Mary Redshaw related her actions at the crime scene. She said that she found the door ajar and went immediately to the vault where she found her husband slumped down in the doorway, his face covered in blood. Other witnesses at the inquest included Mrs. Jane Germano, who said she heard Mary's screams from across the street and went with her back to the crime scene. Mrs. Germano thought that Mr. Redshaw might have had a heart attack. She also tried to find a pulse in the fallen man, but there was none. Edward Vogel also testified, saying he first noticed the gunshot wounds when they were placing the body in the ambulance.

The description of the suspects by witnesses only provided a generalized sketch. One man wearing a tan overcoat, and another man appearing to be an Italian were seen in the getaway car. Other suspects included a man and a woman with a young boy, who were seen driving into town just ahead of the getaway car. The man was described as 35-40 years old, 5'9", and weighing 185 lbs. The female seen with him appeared to be 5'8," weighing 115 lbs. with shoulder-length hair. A small boy, 3-5 years old, was with them when they parked a blue, 1953 Olds in front of the Putnam County Record at 10:30 a.m. Both cars fled the scene shortly after the murder running a stop sign as they sped out of town.

There was no physical evidence to determine the identity of the assailants. The jury could only conclude that John Redshaw died of gunshot wounds by an unknown person or persons. Apparently, he was also struck twice in the head; the impressions were similar to the butt of a pistol.

When the state crime work was completed, a report with the forensic details was sent to the sheriff. It indicated all of the fingerprints found were those of Redshaw except for one print. The bullets were all .38 caliber, and all were fired from a Colt revolver. The time of death was determined to be between

9 and 10 a.m. Norman Hoover of Granville said he saw someone, who looked like Redshaw, seated at his desk at 9:57 a.m.

The owner of the presumed getaway car was W. E. Erickson, who had reported it stolen. He gave his address as 3540 W. 115th St., Chicago. Erickson traveled to Granville on Thursday, Sept. 29 to retrieve his car. State's attorney Boyle told a reporter he had no reason to detain Erickson as a suspect in the homicide, but he said he would question the man anyhow.

The stolen license plates on the Olds were registered for a Dodge owned by Jay Orras of 1446 S. Kenneth St., Chicago. Orras had parked his car at the Hotpoint Manufacturing Co. in Cicero, IL. He noticed the plates were stolen the same day as the Redshaw murder, but did not report the theft until Tuesday. The man's boss gave him an alibi saying he was at work all day on Monday. Boyle and Sheriff Benson theorized that the plates were probably stolen on Sunday night or Monday morning.

When the News-Tribune asked if the FBI would get involved in the murder investigation, they received a negative reply. According to the federal agency, there were two conditions that precluded its involvement. First, there had to be positive evidence that the amount of the theft was over $5,000, and secondly, there would have to be some indication that the stolen property was taken across state lines. As far as the FBI was concerned, neither of these conditions seemed to be evident in this case. Attorney Boyle still hoped that the FBI would take an interest in the case since he believed that the stolen gems were likely taken across state lines.

Boyle later told a News-Tribune reporter it might be impossible to determine the amount of property and money taken. Since Redshaw was found with a jeweler's loupe on his head, Boyle was of the opinion that the murders had posed as customers interested in purchasing diamonds or other gemstones. Redshaw may have even known the individuals, but had his machine gun handy nonetheless. Although it was found unloaded, it might have given pause to any unscrupulous individuals, who posed a threat during any transaction.

In November 2009, Bill Ellena, a Granville resident, provided information supporting the theory that Redshaw probably knew the assailant(s). Ellena said Jack feared that someone might threaten his life. So, when an unfamiliar car parked in front of his McCoy Street office, the astute trader would copy down the car make and license number on a pad of paper, which was hidden from view. When the police checked the list, however, there was no record of the '55 Olds, the presumed getaway car.

Jack was also known to have many business dealings with residents from other states. The state's attorney said he planned to question two out-of-state customers. There were at least 50 potential suspects, who were customers of Redshaw.

Doing business with out-of-towners apparently caused Jack much anxiety. Tonarelli said that Jack always carried a pistol in a shoulder holster and drove a big, black Packard from his house to his office only a couple of blocks away.

Redshaw pictured with his 1937 Packard at his house across from the city park. Although his office was only a short distance from his house, he drove to work in this car. John L. Redshaw collection.

Another close friend of Jack's was Fritz Ballerine. Jack once asked Ballerine, "Why don't you learn the business?" suggesting that he might become a partner. Ballerine later confided he didn't think he could be a success at the trading business. Ballerine also felt that Jack always seemed wary of some of the people coming to trade merchandise with him. Tonarelli confirmed that opinion stating that Jack hid a pistol under his hat on the desk. He was also known to have loaded pistols in his wastebaskets.

Another interesting clue as to the gunmen was revealed in a Feb. 24, 2010 article by Darrell Alleman in the Putnam County Record. He described an interview he had some years earlier with Boyle. The attorney suggested the murder was likely carried out by a criminal gang since the heads of the recovered bullets had an "X" carved into them.

Was Redshaw connected to the underworld as a fence? In Alleman's article, Boyle said he didn't think so.

It was widely assumed the motive for the crime was robbery, but witnesses said uncut gems were found lying in the pool of blood, and the killers did not bother to remove a large diamond ring from the victim's finger nor pilfer the $220 in his wallet.

According to a Nov. 12, 1955 News-Tribune story, there were seven safes in the vault. "The one that was opened by the Trader contained 'the cream' of his jewelry. Among the gems missing is a star sapphire in excess of 43 karats." The stone was valued at over $10,000.

In early November, Theodore L. Link, a reporter for the St. Louis Post-Dispatch, proposed a different motive for Redshaw's murder. He suggested the Granville businessman was one of three recent victims whose deaths might be connected to a large ransom that had mysteriously disappeared.

Two years earlier in September 1953, Carl Austin Hall and Bonnie Emily Brown Heady kidnapped six-year old Bobby Greenlease, the son of Robert Cosgrove Greenlease, a multimillionaire businessman. Posing as the boy's aunt, Heady told Sister Morand at Notre Dame de Sion, a private Catholic school in Kansas City, MO, that Bobby's mother had had a heart attack and asked the nun to release the first grader into her custody. Not thinking of contacting the boy's home first, the nun complied. Heady and Hall fled to Missouri where Hall shot and killed Bobby. Then, the criminals coldly demanded $600,000 for the safe return of the boy, who they had already buried. The father paid the money, which, at that time, was the largest ransom ever paid in U.S. history.

The kidnappers flaunted their ill-gotten wealth and were soon arrested. Justice was swift. Hall and Heady were tried; found guilty; and executed in the Missouri gas chamber in December 1953.

However, the investigation continued because only about half the ransom money was recovered and returned to the family. In April 1954, St. Louis police officer Elmer Dolan and Lt. Louis Shoulders were found guilty of perjury when they told the court they had brought a suitcase containing the ransom money into the police station. Both received prison sentences.

A few of the missing $20 bills were eventually found. In September, one bill was spotted at the Federal Reserve Bank of Chicago. Three more turned up at the Federal Reserve Bank of St. Louis. Another $20 bill was discovered in Minot, N.D. But, these discoveries did not provide a significant trail that would result in the recovery of the missing $303,720.

Link drove to Putnam County to collect information that would support his conspiracy story. He theorized Redshaw might have been killed by individuals, who believed the ransom money was hidden in the Granville vault. In his article Link wrote, "There have been indications someone believed that all or some of the $10 and $20 ransom bills had been left" in Redshaw's vault. However, State's Attorney Durley Boyle told Link that his theory was "absolutely groundless." According to the Putnam County Record, Mary was "not only unhappy but extremely indignant toward the St. Louis reporter." She asked the Record to print the following: "There is absolutely no truth to her husband and the Greenlease case money." Boyle told a News-Tribune reporter that the St. Louis newspaper account was a "reporter's dream."

The Redshaw murder frightened a number of residents. In an October 2009 interview, Bonucchi confided that Mary Redshaw told him that she had received phone calls following her husband's death intimating the investigation should be ended immediately. Mary never revealed who made the calls, but she did ask Bonucchi to install bars on the windows of her house. Others said that Mary had become something of a recluse and did not venture out of her house very often. Tonarelli also worried about repercussions, He told the Putnam County state's attorney, "Durley, don't call me (to testify)."

According to Alleman's account in the Record, Boyle and Sheriff Benson traveled to Chicago to question some of Jack's customers and known jewel thieves. Apparently, those interviews caused a lieutenant from the Chicago police department to contact Boyle and Benson advising them it would be a good idea to "go back to Putnam County and forget the case or they might end up like Redshaw."

If it was an ordinary robbery, the question remained. Why did trays of precious stones and hundreds of valuable silver coins apparently remain untouched? According to John L. Redshaw, Jack's nephew, the family maintained Jack's brothers, Ervin and Roy Redshaw, removed the gems from the vault shortly after the murder. An auction was later held to dispose of the warehouse property. Jack had planned to record an inventory of his holdings, but no list was found. Without an inventory, it was impossible to determine what was stolen.

In June 1956, attorney Durley Boyle, who conducted an inventory of Jack Redshaw property, set its value at $85,211.33. Of that, 520 rifles were assessed at over $4,000. One asset, valued at $1,750, was the famous "Hinkey Dink" Kenna's diamond star, named for Michael Kenna, a Chicago alderman and political boss with ties to the Capone mob. Kenna died in 1946. A little over $6,000 was attributed to the musical instruments and artwork. Redshaw's 1955 Cadillac was valued at $3,200. Not included in the appraisal were 316 watches, 318 diamonds, and other jewelry. "We know that Redshaw had a collection of unset diamonds of fabulous value, most of which are missing and would be extremely difficult to trace," Boyle said. It appeared the perpetrators had pulled off the perfect crime.

Jack Redshaw left everything to his wife and daughter. There were enough items in the warehouse to keep Mary busy for the rest of her life. She continued to operate the trading business on a limited basis because she had no idea of the value of some of the items.
Interior of Redshaw warehouse. John L. Redshaw photo collection.

Occasionally, a visitor came to the office. Mary would often offer them a copy of the one book that kept her spirits up, "With God All things Are Possible."
Mary Redshaw kept this photo just above the phone over which Jack did much of his trading. John L. Redshaw photo collection.

The murder remains unsolved to this day. According to Cathy Oliveri, the circuit clerk, there were no records found of the murder in the Hennepin courthouse in 2009. Nor were there any records of the murder in Sheriff Kevin Doyle's office. Durley Boyle, who may have had a better idea of what happened that fateful day, died in 2009.

ENJOYING A WHITE CHRISTMAS

In spite of the negative news of major fires, continued gambling raids, and the growing Cold War tensions, the year ended on a positive note. Children in the Tri-Cities had a wonderful program on Christmas Eve thanks to the continued Big Hearts program. The management of the Majestic Theater in LaSalle opened their doors to over 900 children. Buses were used to bring children from distant locations in Peru, LaSalle, and Oglesby. The movie portion of the show included cartoons, and a feature film, "Lost in Alaska." There was also live musical entertainment. Through it all, the local Boy Scouts helped to supervise the children and pass out bags of candy, fruit, and nuts.

While the children were being entertained, the Teamsters union distributed toys. Under the Christmas trees the next day, little girls would find dolls dressed in clothing sewn by local women in the months before the holiday.

There was also entertainment for the adults for the holiday. "White Christmas" was playing at the Majestic and the Peru theaters.

Advertisement from the Dec. 24, 1955 edition of the News-Tribune.

1956
THE NEW STANDARD IN ROCK ISLAND SERVICE

Whereas the *Jet Rocket* "demo" train only had one coach, the train coming in February 1956 would have a combined baggage-passenger car followed by a parlor car with a dining section seating 32 passengers and a beverage section seating another 12 passengers. There would also be two more coaches. The total capacity was 306 – 15 more than the standard *Rocket* carried.

The big day finally arrived. An official christening was held in Peoria on Saturday, Feb. 11, 1956. Miss Mary Louise Neumiller, daughter of Caterpillar chairman and Rock Island board member Louis Neumiller, had the honor of breaking a bottle of champagne over the nose of the Jet Rocket No. 1. The revolutionary train arrived in LaSalle at 3:56 p.m. Two trainmen from Bureau were aboard, Grover Kane, the conductor, and Joseph Martin, a brakeman. Stops were made in Ottawa, Morris, and Joliet before reaching Chicago at about 5:30 in the evening as scheduled.

The No. 1 *Jet Rocket* arrives in LaSalle.

Finally, a regular *Jet Rocket* schedule was developed. Starting on April 29, 1956, the No. 501 train would leave Chicago at 9:55 a.m. and arrive in Joliet about 40 minutes later. From there, it was a 20-minute ride to Morris. The *Jet Rocket* was due to arrive in Ottawa at 11:17 a.m., another 20-minute ride. It pulled into the LaSalle depot about 15 minutes later. The 501 reached Peoria at 12:30 in the afternoon. Another train, the 502, would leave Chicago in the evening at 5:30 p.m. and make the usual stops with the exception of Ottawa to arrive in LaSalle at a little after 7 p.m.

Jet Rocket trains left Peoria twice a day. Train 502 left Peoria at 6:30 a.m. Passengers in LaSalle would board at 7:26 a.m. Additional stops were made at Ottawa at 7:41 a.m. and Morris at 8:02 am. Arrival in Chicago was scheduled for 9:10 a.m. Train 504 departed from Peoria at 2 p.m. and stopped in LaSalle at about 3:30. That train arrived in the Windy City at 4:45 p.m. each day.

Unfortunately, once the *Jet Rockets* went into service, problems became apparent. The air suspension failed at speeds above 60 mph; the rubber bellows on the single axle trucks completely compressed. The power car wasn't easy to service. Electrical components were in the cab under the nose. Frequently, the train failed to stop because of a failure of the automotive-type drum brakes, which tended to overheat and crack.

Installing a single shoe, clasp-type brake, solved one problem on the *Jet Rockets*. The rubber-cushioned shock absorbers were also removed from the prototypes. Photo by author.

Problems continued to manifest themselves in disturbing ways. Because of its light weight, the train didn't activate block signals when the train rolled by. This created a potential collision with other trains because the signal remained green while the *Jet Rocket* was still on the tracks. Using a higher voltage didn't solve the problem either. The train did activate the higher voltage signal but so did rain and fog. Signal lights glowed red whenever there was excessive moisture even though there was no train on the tracks. Another problem was the tendency of the light-weight train to bounce on tracks. Some passengers were tossed around and even injured. Their coffee cups splashed uncontrollably. The train was also too small. The lounge held only 20 seats compared to 40 seats on the standard trains. One novel feature was a closed-circuit television system. Passengers in the lounge car were terrified with the view of near-misses with pedestrians, school buses, and other vehicles as the *Jet Rocket* sped by crossings at 90 mph. The crew had to disable the television to calm the passengers. It was only a matter of time before Rock Island management was compelled to pull the futuristic train from its fleet.

A RARE TOUR OF WESTCLOX

Factories don't usually open their doors for thousands of visitors, but for two days, April 25-26, invitations were extended to the families of the 4,000 Westclox employees. Even with that limit, the number of guests was far more than the number expected by management. Cars filled the L-P High School practice field parking lot. Buses were used to take the throngs to the plant. Once inside, the crowds were so thick the electric trucks used to move parts could not get through the aisles. Some visitors came from New York and Indiana for this rare opportunity. Female visitors on the three-quarter mile tour were given roses at the entrance. At the end of the tour, food was provided along with prizes for many of the lucky ticket holders. On the tours, visitors could see how timing mechanisms were assembled. By the end of the day on Thursday, the organizers ran out of food because of the unexpected size of the turnout. The crowds exceeded the planners' expectations by 47 percent. M.C. Budlong, general manager, said, "We were swamped on Thursday afternoon and glad of it." There was much interest in seeing the operations, that produced very small parts for projects like bomb fuses for the military.

WATCHING FOR RUSSIAN BOMBERS

One railroad employee was interested in watching for something more sinister than bomb fuses. Richard McDowell, the IC depot agent in Oglesby, volunteered for the Ground Observer Corps in April 1956, replacing the previous agent, K. E. Nunn. When asked for the reason he joined the GOC,

McDowell replied, "I believe the work is important. It just might prevent an enemy from getting the jump on us. If war ever comes, it seems quite likely that enemy planes will invade the skies. One of the main reasons the corps is important is that radar won't pick up low flying planes. And radar can miss some high flying planes too." McDowell typically only spent his afternoons watching for Russian aircraft. During the day, he was responsible for checking IC freight cars in the Lehigh and Marquette yards. However, when there were national alerts in the summer, he said he spent the entire day spotting planes. According to GOC guidelines, he had only six minutes to report to Chicago; otherwise, his report was worthless.

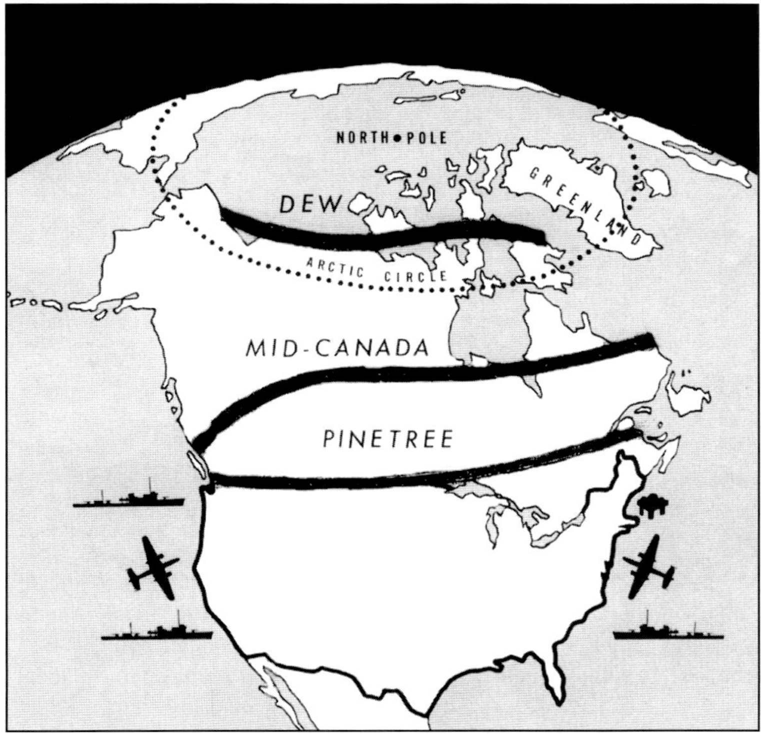

Badly undermanned in 1956, the GOC network was gradually being supplemented by radar units in Canada and the Arctic. Three lines of radar dishes made up the Pine Tree Line, the Mid-Canada Line and the Distant Early Warning (DEW) Line.

During 1952, a training site was established for radar technicians in the Streator area. The Columbia and Plumb hotels were used for sleeping quarters for the men training to become "radicians" (radar technicians). Photo submitted by Gary Spears.

The training site was located five miles southwest of Streator north of Route 17. Site construction was carried out during 1955-57. Training continued until decades later when most of the equipment was removed. Distant photos of the training site were released to the local press in August 1956. After training at Streator, the men were assigned to one of the 58 sites on the DEW line. Photo contributed by Robert Young, who trained at Streator and served at a DEW line station. Because of the classified nature of the work, no photos of the interior of the buildings were allowed.

Three of the men who worked on the DEW line were Larry Hrasch, Jack Berckemeyer, and Ed Majercin of Streator. They met in 2010 to reminisce about their work on the radar sites in the Arctic. They were among the hundreds of men known as the "Guardians of the North."

Training in Streator followed a set routine. After breakfast, the men boarded Air Force busses for the ride from Streator to their classes, which lasted 8-10 weeks according to Larry Hrasch. The men had to have security clearances at the "Secret" level to pass through the gate, which was manned by a private security guard service. Classes were conducted by civilians. There were 8-10 men in each class dealing with radar and communications. In addition, "every student went through weather school," said Hrasch. Jack Berckemeyer was one of the instructors at the Streator site. During the radar simulations, radar operators tracked three targets at a time. At the end of the training, there were three days of live exercises when the console operators would track small planes flying from the Streator airport to the area around the radar site.

There were more people involved besides those manning the DEW line radar consoles. Ed Majercin trained for his job in Detroit. He was a roving diesel mechanic for the power generators. While working between the remote sites, where only 4-5 men were stationed, he was able to visit some of the Eskimo villages in Alaska. Hrasch worked in logistics on the DEW line in Greenland.

The DEW line radar equipment in the Arctic was very similar to that at the Streator training site. Inside the large dome was the FPS-19 radar unit. Two antennas were attached back-to-back and rotated on a central pivot. The four dish antennas on the ground were used to communicate between DEW line stations. Two of the antennas faced east and two faced west. At the Streator training site, only two of these antennas were built. Photo by Brian Jeffrey.

Equipment like this was used to train men at the Streator facility in air-to-ground and ground-to-ground communication. Brian Jeffrey, who trained at Streator and served at the CAM-4 site in 1960-61, contributed this photo.

About 150 men completed the training program at the Streator installation every year. Each trainee received $400 a month and a living allowance. Upon completion of the course, the radicians were sent to the DEW line stations. According to Ed Majercin, the pay was $1,050 a month with a $1,500 bonus after completing an 18-month assignment. Leave time was allowed as well. Not everyone could endure the harsh Arctic conditions for that length of time. However, others enjoyed the high pay and signed up for several tours of duty.

The men, who trained at Streator on equipment like this, watched their DEW line radar screens for Russian and American planes. The two radarscopes showed signals from the two antennas in the radome. The radar operator was seated at the right scope watching targets from the low-beam antenna tracking planes at low altitude. The scope at the left was for the high-beam antenna tracking at higher altitudes. During a crisis situation, there would be two operators watching both scopes. The goal was to provide NORAD with a four-hour advance warning of a pending Soviet attack. Photo contributed by Brian Jeffrey.

Still standing in a farm field is one of the two lateral antennas used to communicate between stations on the DEW line. At one time, another small intermediate-range station was built north of Utica. Photo by author.

The abandoned guard shack, entrance gate, and barbed wire fence are situated on the perimeter of the site, which was closed in the early 1980's. Other buildings for equipment maintenance and console and communicaitons training deteriorate more every year. Photo by author.

This building at the Streator training site was used as the mess hall and classrooms for the weather classes. Photo by author.

This structure once supported the huge dome, which covered the radar antennas. Under the platform was the transmitting equipment. The antennas were dismanteled and sent to Pin, ME. The consoles were sent to Colorado Springs.
Photo by author.

The DEW line installations were an important part of the Cold War defense for Canada and the United States. In July 1956, a mock Soviet attack on 73 major American cities and nine Canadian cities was played out. The simulation included H-bomb attacks on Skokie, IL and Chicago Heights. The role of the Tri-Cities in these annual exercises was to provide simulated assistance to those evacuating the attack sites.

Gambling crimes had become less of a problem in the Illinois Valley, but occasionally the police conducted a raid. For instance, at noon on April 27, Police Chief Walter Nijak and three deputies visited Happy's Tavern in LaSalle. At one end of the bar, they found a cigar box with a note pad with some memos. One read, "Sixty-Two at Sportsman Jr. Orlandini 3 win." Another cryptic note read, "Sixth-two-4th at Sportsman - Mushy 2 win." Envelopes filled with various amounts of cash bearing the names of "Jiggle," and "Ralph" were also found. There were some tip ticket stubs with the winners' names, Joop, Tony Miller, and Ralph Tidabeck, and twelve baseball boards. The police arrested Ciro Baschiere, the proprietor of the bar at 1678 St. Vincent's, and Rudolph Hrovat, who was charged with possession of gambling equipment. Both confessed their crimes to the police magistrate, Francis Gielow, and paid a total of $400 in fines.

On Saturday, April 14, a $20,000 jewel theft of diamonds was reported by a Chicago salesman while at the Plumb Hotel in Streator. While he went to dinner, Rudolph Hendrickson left a case containing the gems at the hotel lobby with the clerk. When he returned, the case was missing. The clerk, Frank Morrison, said he was never told what was in the case and only stepped away from the desk twice for a short time. Pinkerton detectives were called to investigate.

Another robbery occurred on June 5. A lone gunman robbed the First National Bank of Triumph, located twelve miles northeast of LaSalle. The bandit waited until the employees returned from lunch at 1 p.m. before entering the bank. He brandished a black-handled pistol and shouted, "This is a heist." The cashier, Everett Christopher; and three other employees, the assistant cashier, Mrs. Arlena Ridge of Mendota; and Mrs. Dean Foote and Mrs. Virginia Shultz, the bookkeepers, were ordered to lie face down on the floor and to cross their arms and legs. The robber was apologetic as he tied up the women with black wire. Then, the cigar-smoking bandit even asked Christopher where they kept the ashtrays before ordering him to open the safe in the vault. After binding Christopher with wire, the robber began stuffing a white canvas bag with bills. His work was interrupted when a customer, Maurice Olsen, entered the bank. He was also tied up. Moments later, Olsen's father, Oliver Olsen, entered the bank. When ordered to lie down behind the counter, the startled customer fled into the street with the gun-wielding robber chasing him. Instead of shooting the elder Olsen, the bandit returned to retrieve his bag left on the counter filled with $14,000. The robber had overlooked the stacks of coins on the counters and missed $4,700 in bills hidden out of sight in the

cashiers' cages. The First National Bank of Triumph, where the robbery took place, is a gutted building today. The Gehant Bank of Triumph located next to the old bank now serves the village. Photo by author.

The robber's escape was almost comical as the getaway car, a grey 1950-51 model with red wheels, sputtered on the first two attempts to start the vehicle. Mr. L. J. Seiling, manager of the local elevator, came into the bank and untied the captives while another elevator employee informed the Ottawa police of the holdup. Roadblocks were established on the roads leading away from Triumph.

Witnesses described the bank robber as about 30 years old, 5'6", and weighing about 145 pounds. He was wearing a light-colored suit and hat with a black band. Identification of the license plate added more information. The car was registered to Gilbert Owens of 4039 W. Armitage in Chicago, and had been purchased three days earlier from a Chicago car dealer. The distinctive red wheels on the car made it quite noticeable to a local farmer, Edward Packenham, who saw it speeding away in a westerly direction at 100 mph. Mrs. Young the wife of the pastor of the Waltham Presbyterian Church, and Mabel Chapin watched as the car spun completely around and slid into a ditch at an intersection near the church. The driver drove out of the ditch and continued in his high-speed escape. Mrs. John Slingsby and Lester Roax also saw the car as it passed them traveling east at 2:15 p.m. The police lost the trail at the Wallace Township School. One possible clue was a map, the police found marked with rural roads from Bureau County to Triumph. The investigation continued, and the bandit was captured in 1957.

Another bank holdup took place at the Sheridan State Bank on Monday afternoon, Sept. 24. This time the crime was quickly solved.

After his capture, Fred Jovanovich, 37, of Ottawa provided the details of his crime to Sheriff Edward Lambert, Ottawa Police Chief Walter Keim, and the FBI. Armed with a 9 mm automatic pistol, Jovanovich said he entered the bank and walked up to Victor E. Meyer, Handing him a paper bag he said, "Fill it full." After the bank's cash drawer was emptied of $7,012, the robber moved to the next teller, H.C. Price. Jovanovich told Price to extend his hands and then tied them with wire. The bandit also tied the hands of Meyer and Mrs. Thomas Morey, a bookkeeper. He ordered the three bank employees to move into the vault. Jovanovich did not close the vault door completely after Price told him there was no ventilation.

Jovanovich made good his escape but was spotted by Mrs. Louise Robinson, who thought the man looked suspicious, and copied down the license of the green and white getaway car. The bank employees were already freeing themselves, and the police were quickly notified. The license plate number was traced to Jovanovich's home at 1016 Polk St. An Ottawa police officer, Donald Rexroat, made the arrest as the robber pulled up to the house. By about 3:25 p.m., they were at the police station, and Jovanovich confessed. He said he had planned the robbery for a month because he was in debt and had lost money gambling. He also told the officers where he had stashed the stolen money. Officer Russell Latino and Deputy George Novotney found a paper bag containing the money under the driver's seat of the car exactly as Jovanovich confessed. The bank employees identified the robber.

While the Sheridan bank robbery was solved within an hour, the Triumph robbery took a little longer. There had been few clues to the Triumph crime. The gunman's getaway car, a grey Hudson, was found abandoned on Rt. 29 north of Peoria shortly after the robbery.

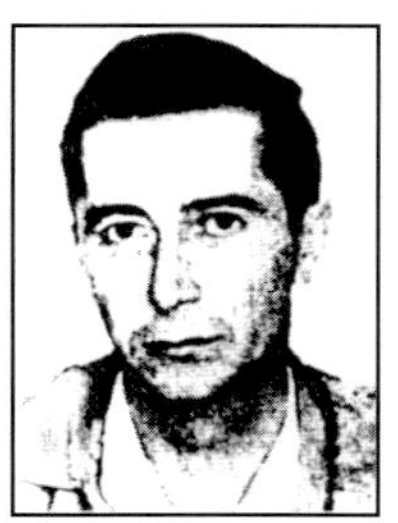

The perpetrator, was discovered to be a 38-year old Dixon businessman, Howard J. Hansen. On Mar. 25, 1957, the FBI found him in Chicago and charged him with five bank robberies. His thefts amounted to over $55,000. A native of Princeton, he was armed with a .32 caliber pistol but made no attempt to flee when he was confronted at the Flying Saucer tavern on Archer Ave. He confessed to the Triumph robbery and four other ones: two in Illinois, the Poplar Grove State Bank and the Farmers State Bank in Danforth and two in Wisconsin, the Pewaukee State Bank in Brookfield and the State Bank of Lodi in Dane. Hansen used the money from the bank robberies to open a radiator repair service in Dixon.

On May 13, 1957, District Court Judge William J. Campbell found Hansen guilty of the robberies in Triumph and Poplar Grove. He handed down a sentence of 10 years in the penitentiary to run concurrently for those Illinois robberies. Hansen still faced charges for the three other bank robberies.

One more major crime occurred on Dec. 13. The Treasure Chest jewelry store in LaSalle was burglarized. The thieves stole an assortment of over 200 watches and rings, which were valued at $13,000 by the owners, Arnold Faerber and Ray Kramarsic. According to the owners, the stolen items were among the most valuable items in the store indicating it was likely a crime committed by professionals.

1957

FLAMES ENGULF OLD PRINCETON BANK BUILDING

The new year had barely begun before a major fire swept through the old First National Bank building at 636 S. Main, Princeton. On Sunday afternoon, Jan. 13, Princeton firemen together with fire departments from Wyanet and Tiskilwa battled the flames for three hours in near-zero weather. Most of the estimated $75,000 in damages occurred in the structure owned by Mrs. Charles Gross. It was felt that the fire started in the attic where there was a furnace used to heat a seven-room third floor apartment occupied by Ludwig Holdeman, a cook at the Ranch House Restaurant in Bureau. The lower floors, occupied by the Alma Magnuson dress shop and the office of the Trimble law firm and State's Attorney Donald C. Martin were also damaged by water and smoke. Firemen also worked to stop the flames from reaching adjoining buildings. These included the Ben Franklin store, the G.E. Lund and W.L. Phelan optometry shops, and the Landahl store.

Several months later, another fire swept through the downtown area of LaSalle. The inferno, which was discovered in the early morning hours of Apr. 23, was concentrated on the Beardsley Paint and Wallpaper store in the 500 block of First Street, an area of numerous small businesses. The fire was believed to have started on the second floor in some cartons used for mixing paint. Smoke damage spread to the Dimas Restaurant, Koehler's, Akerman Optical, the Chicago Motor Club office, the Singer sewing machine shop, and Louise Haley's Millinery store.

MORE THAN FIRES TO BE SEEN

While fires always drew big crowds, a month later, there was another spectacle watched by hundreds of boat fans along the river. Alerted by the News-Tribune that a big cargo carrier was on its way up the Illinois River, the crowd lined the riverbanks on Feb. 11 to watch the passage of the 590-foot *Joseph S. Young* being pushed by the *Larry Turner*.

The "River Traffic" report of the arrival time in the paper was in error by over three hours at Spring Valley, but diehard boat watchers sat in their cars or on the ground in the frigid weather awaiting the arrival. The wait was even longer for those at Starved Rock lock. The ship, built at the Baltimore shipyards, narrowly slipped into the locks with its 68-foot beam. It had taken about 22 hours to navigate the river from Peoria to Peru and finally arrived in Chicago on Feb. 14. The ship's next destination was Manitowoc, WI.

The ore ship *Joseph S. Young.* Digital image from the Fr. Edward J. Dowling, S. J., Marine Historical Collection, University of Detroit Mercy.

NATIONAL SECURITY TAKES PRIORITY

Unions have their place, but military needs came first. In March 1957, Westclox was awarded a major contract for the production of a new type of timing device for mortar shells. Soldiers had been wounded and killed with the old WWII rounds when they detonated too soon after being fired. Peru workers were busy producing the 21 parts needed for the timer, which would delay detonation for at least three-four seconds after clearing the launching tube. Actual assembly of the fuses took place in Philadelphia. Millions of the new fuses were needed to replace old ammunition. The problem was that Westclox union workers had gone on strike over issues regarding raises and seniority.

The strike went on for seven weeks until July 22, when 20 of the workers went back to work making parts for the fuses. Federal judge William Campbell responded to a request by the National Labor Review Board to order the members of Local 12573 back to work since the union had not followed proper procedures prior to the walkout. The government contract called for the Westclox parts for 66,000 fuses to be assembled in the Frankfort Arsenal in Philadelphia.

The strike came to an end on Monday, July 29, after negotiations between management and labor had resolved their differences. A vote on the agreement could not be taken before the workers returned to the Peru plant. The union settled for a 6¢ raise, retroactive to July, and a similar raise in 1958.

Cold War needs also resulted in a military contract being awarded to the H. D. Conkey Co. in Mendota. The company manufactured bombs for the military in WWII, so it was not surprising that the company received a $1,320,000 order to manufacture a new practice bomb for the Navy.

Labor negotiations were unresolved in a regional walkout at 60 cement plants including Lehigh in Oglesby and Alpha in LaSalle. The strike, begun in June, was in its second week and spreading. The workers at Dixon's Medusa plant stopped production during early July. Nationwide there were about 150 cement plants. It appeared hopeful that the members of the United Cement Lime and Gypsum Workers Union would accept the offer of a 13.6¢ average wage increase made by the Marquette Cement Manufacturing Co. One of the sticking points was the practice of subcontracting union work.

CELEBRATIONS EASE TENSIONS

While labor problems lingered on into the summer, there was also time to relax and focus on the good things in life. The Tenth Annual Sweet Corn Festival in Mendota attracted 26,000, the biggest turnout ever. The two-day event featured a parade downtown led by the marines, the Mendota Sea Explorers, and representatives of three veterans' posts. Local high school and grade school bands marched along with the Moose Heart Girls Drum and Bugle Corps, the Mendota Accordion Band, and a band from Dixon. Among the 100 marching units and commercial and organizational floats was the Mendota Hospital Auxiliary, which took first place in its division. The festival would not be complete without some children's contests. Charles Robinson and Richie Lee Lind of

Mendota took first place in the corn-eating contest for the kids 6-8 years old. The winners in the sweet corn throwing contest included Ellen and Adele Balanco (DePue), Judy Maher (Peru), Cheryl Roux (Ottawa), Roger Thompson (Dayton), and Larry Snyder (Mendota).

There were also some special events for 1957. One of the new developments, long awaited in the Tri-Cities, was the opening of a new shopping area north of Route 6 in Peru. The Midway Plaza, which included twelve new stores, had a grand opening Aug. 15.

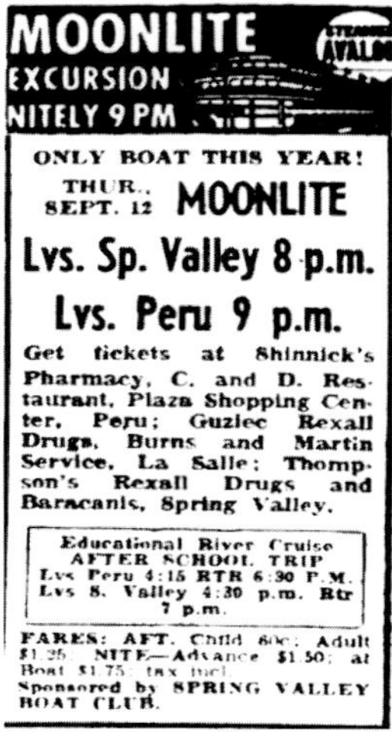

The steamer *Avalon* made a return trip up the Illinois River to offer rides for only 60¢ for children and $1.75 for adults on the evening excursion.

The crowds at the Les-Buzz dance hall enjoyed the rock and roll music of Bill Haley and the Comets. Their hit songs included "Rock Around the Clock," and "Shake, Rattle, & Roll." Tickets to the Spring Valley show were only $2.50.
Dick Verucchi collection.

THE JET ROCKET IS GROUNDED

On May 11, 1957, the controversial Peoria *Jet Rocket* was scheduled to be replaced by the standard Rock Island *Rockets*. Service would be upgraded to include a full-sized diner and parlor car. The final run through the Illinois Valley occurred on Aug. 20, 1957. The *Jet Rocket* stopped at the LaSalle-Peru depot at 7:26 a.m. on the last trip to Chicago.

The *Jet Rocket* is now only a museum curiosity in the St. Louis Museum of Transportation. Photo by author.

The older and more reliable Rock Island *Rockets* continued to carry passengers from Peoria to Chicago through the decade.

The Rock Island RR decided there were too many problems trying to operate the train at the optimum high speed between Peoria and Chicago. Instead of scrapping the futuristic train, however, management decided to use the train on the slower commuter runs into Chicago. The problem-ridden *Jet Rockets* were still used on the shorter Joliet-Chicago route, where high speed was not a priority.

TENSION AND TROUBLES RETURN

The good times could not last forever. On Sept. 20, a series of suspicious fires broke out almost simultaneously in Seneca. The alarm came in at 2 a.m. Clifford Brown the police chief ran to his squad car only to find one of his tires slashed. The Seneca, Morris, and Marseilles fire departments all responded. One damaged building was the two-story structure used for the Seneca State Bank and the Masonic Hall. In addition, the James Marshall Garage, housing antiques, was consumed, and the Dunn Co-Op elevator and seed house were burned. Just as the flames were put out at the Dunn building, another fire broke out at a barn owned by A. B. Clark. The bank was heavily damaged, but the contents of the vault were intact. The very next day, there was another fire at the Prairie State Oil Co. office near 16 oil storage tanks. The flames were quickly extinguished. It was surmised that this was not the work of an arsonist as was the case in the previous night's fires, but rather, it was likely caused by an overheated stove.

On Oct. 29, a fire destroyed 25 cars and trucks at the Ottawa Body Co. Even before the Ottawa fire department arrived on the scene, flames covered the roof, and smoke filled the interior. Fortunately, the northeasterly winds, kept the fire from spreading to a nearby gas station. Employees of the Carlson Desoto Motor Co. were able to move the vehicles in their used car lot just to the east of the body shop located next to the building. The Broadus and Johnson auto accessories shop was gutted. The owners lost all of their equipment. Their loss was estimated at $7,000. One couple, Mr. and Mrs. Walter Miner, who rented an apartment in the building, lost their car, which was stored in the building, and all of their household possessions.

The quick response of fire departments from Naplate and Streator to assist the men from Ottawa, kept the inferno from spreading to other car dealerships on the block. The fire was under control within an hour, but the men stayed on the scene until noon dousing the smoldering remains.

OTTAWA SOLDIER TRIED BY JAPANESE

One of the disturbing stories making headlines through the entire year revolved around Army Specialist 3/c William S. Girard. The Japanese government accused the young soldier from Ottawa of firing an empty cartridge case from a grenade launcher causing the death of Mrs. Naka Sakai, 46, a Japanese civilian, who was collecting scrap metal from the firing range on Jan. 30, 1957.

The legal wrangling over issues, such as the jurisdictional right of the Japanese courts to prosecute American soldiers, delayed the case until the US Supreme Court ruled 8-0 in July there was no bar to the right of the Japanese courts to hear the case.

The formal trial began on Aug. 26. Subsequent hearings were scheduled through September and October.

At the trial, the Japanese prosecutor charged that Girard had intentionally lured Mrs. Sakai onto the firing range. It was claimed the soldier had been throwing spent cartridges into the field range thereby enticing Japanese scavengers to collect the brass.

The three-judge panel ruled in November that Girard was indeed guilty. The judgment was a three-year suspended prison sentence with probation for a fourth year. He was also ordered to pay $20 for the court costs of the witnesses. He might have received a more severe punishment of a prison term of 2-15 years. However, the court's presiding judge said, "the court's job is not to sentence a man to jail; it is to try to keep him out of jail so that he will reflect on how to become a better man." The ordeal was over, and Girard planned to leave Japan with his Japanese wife and return to the U.S.

THE SPACE AGE BEGINS

The launching of the first space satellite on Oct. 4 at the remote Tyuratam launch site of the Russians in Kazakhstan heightened the growing competition between the US and USSR. While the event would seem to have only interest to the scientific community and the armed forces, there was an immediate civilian reaction in the Illinois Valley.

The small satellite, not much bigger than a beach ball, was broadcasting a very distinct signal as it traveled around the earth every 90 minutes. Two university students from the area,

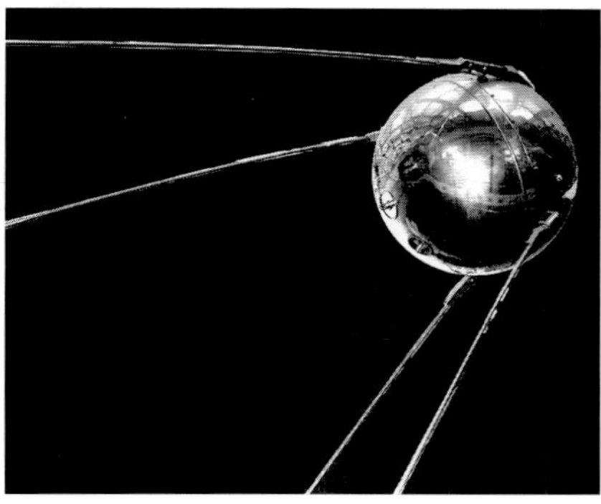

Ken Piletic from LaSalle and Raymond Sarwinski from Peru, were anxious to hear the transmissions. As members of a scientific team at the University of Illinois in Champaign-Urbana, they began tracking the satellite and recording the radio signal. The tapes they made were forwarded to the US Navy for analysis. Ernest Stuart, one of the local ham radio operators in LaSalle was also listening to the beep-beep signals being transmitted. Charles Ford was listening to his Philco shortwave radio and picked up the signal on two different frequencies. Ed Reminh of LaSalle also picked up the transmissions. Soon, hams throughout the Illinois Valley were listening to the Russian satellite. Radio Moscow helped the world to learn about their achievement and broadcast the exact frequencies for ham radio operators around the world.

The local schools were quick to develop student interest in the Soviet accomplishment. At Jefferson School, a News-Tribune photographer took a picture of three seventh graders in Jean Feeny's class. David Gearhart, Joseph Nolasco, and Richard Morrow were engaged in their studies about the Russian satellite simply known as Sputnik.

Within a month, there was another major space achievement for the Russians. They had placed a dog, Laika, in orbit around the earth in Sputnik II.

According to the Soviet press, Laika had spent several days in the space capsule before the launch. There was no provision to return the dog alive. Laika reportedly died after a short time from heat and stress. Soviet government photo.

Floyd Sarwinski of LaSalle confirmed the Soviet space accomplishment. As a member of the Illinois Valley Radio Club, he had been monitoring the 40-megacycle band and heard the heartbeat of the dog being broadcast back to the Soviet ground crew. Working with Andrew Baginski, the two hams listened to the distinct signals of the dog's heartbeat. They also heard the transmission "beeps" of Sputnik II on the 20-megacycle band.

Three individuals in Ottawa reported actually seeing the spacecraft at 5:46 a.m. as it rose above the southwestern horizon. Paul Davis spotted it with his telescope. "It was very clear. I thought at first it might be an airplane, but it moved too quickly. It left no streak or vapor trail," he told a Republican Times reporter. Davis, who had heard the beeping signals of Sputnik I on his shortwave radio, also tuned in to the signals coming from Sputnik II. "It was much stronger and clearer than Sputnik I," he said. Davis confirmed the radio signals with another ham in Hull, England. Both agreed the signal coming from Sputnik II was stronger than that from the first Russian satellite.

Vernon Stark said he ventured out to get a glimpse of the Russian satellite at the same time. "It was right on schedule as given in the newspaper reports on Tuesday." Stark wanted to have a witness to his sighting since there had been many unconfirmed UFO sightings in the past. He spotted George Dodd, a milkman making his rounds, and called his attention to the bright object, which moved across the sky for about two minutes until it went below the horizon again.

Stark's desire for verification was a smart move. On Nov. 5, the night before the Sputnik II sighting, sky watchers from Wisconsin to Missouri reported triangular and football-shaped UFO's in colors ranging from blue-green to red and yellow. These were explained as atmospheric disturbances.

At the LaSalle library, Miss Tessie Yopp realized there would be many requests for material on missiles and space. Books, such as "Frontier to Space," and "Discovery of the Universe," were organized into a special display.

The American effort to launch a satellite was assigned to the Navy. The Vanguard satellite, which measured six inches in diameter and weighed a little more than three pounds, was destroyed in a fiery explosion on the launch pad.

The remains of the TV-3 Vanguard satellite are on display at the National Air and Space Museum.

NASA photo.

The destruction of the rocket attempting to launch the Vanguard satellite was captured in this US Navy photo on Dec. 6, 1957.

The launch of the much larger Sputnik II satellite increased concerns of American military leaders. If a dog could be placed in orbit, why not a man or a nuclear bomb?

Once again, Cold War fears encouraged civil defense efforts in the Illinois Valley. Curtis Clay, the Civil Defense director for LaSalle-Peru, emphasized the importance of understanding that in the event of a nuclear war, LaSalle County was expected to handle an influx of as many as 750,000 evacuees from the Chicago area. In addition to the need to increase food and medical supplies and to determine shelter locations, more local volunteers were needed to fill the roles of auxiliary police and firemen, air raid wardens, and radiological monitors.

He also pointed out that radioactive fallout could easily affect the entire state. Basement fallout shelters would provide a 90 percent reduction in the danger of exposure.

The CONELRAD emergency broadcast system, which was created in March 1951, provided information locally over WLPO. All FM stations were required to shut down, and listeners were asked to tune in to the official government announcements on 640 kcs. and 1240 kcs.

Government posters like this one were designed to help Americans understand their roles in the event of a nuclear war. Every new radio was marked with two triangles on the frequency band to indicate where official information would be broadcast.

This Motorola DS9660B radio was specifically designed to alert users of a Conelrad alert. Commercial stations and amateur "hams" were required to have radios similar to this to receive alerts and cease broadcasting during an alert.

The CONELRAD system was designed to prevent enemy bombers from homing in on specific broadcast stations. It also provided the public with two specific frequencies where emergency information would be transmitted. The system became obsolete with the advent of ICBM's and evolved into the Emergency Broadcast System in 1963.

On Dec. 8, 1957, a film titled "A Day Called X" was broadcast on CBS-TV. Narrated by Glenn Ford, it portrayed the reaction of civilians in Portland, Oregon after hearing a CONELRAD alert of a Russian attack.

Official black and yellow signs were posted on public buildings, schools, and businesses to indicate where people should seek shelter in the event of a nuclear attack.

The emphasis on civil defense was also stressed in schools. Sears, Roebuck, and Co. donated Geiger counters across the country. One of these radiation detectors was given to L-P High School. Orville Bauer, the physics instructor, demonstrated to his students how it was used to detect radioactive material.

1958
THE SPACE RACE TIGHTENS

In spite of the initial failure to place the Vanguard satellite into orbit, the American space program showed success in the early months of 1958. On Jan. 31, the Army

placed Explorer I into orbit, and in March, the Navy's Vanguard satellite was successfully launched. For local hams, it was another opportunity to tune in with their radios. Beyond that, few people realized that local firms were supplying some of the parts for the Vanguard launch. Westclox was one of the subcontractors as was Eicor, which furnished the dynamotors needed for the second stage of the three-stage rocket.

Explorer I launch on Jan. 31. NASA photo.

THE IC AND SUBLETTE TO THE RESCUE

Illinois residents could always count on one or more snowstorms each winter. That was especially true in 1958. In late January, the entire Midwest from Kansas and Missouri up through Iowa and Illinois was blanketed in snow. While high winds and a snowfall of 6-14 inches caused a serious drifting problem on highways in the states to the southwest of Illinois, the warmer temperatures – just above freezing – resulted in a wet, heavy snow covering roads and cars with snow and slush in the Land of Lincoln. Salt trucks in the Tri-Cities were covering the highways, but there were still car accidents and vehicles stuck in ditches. Most local events were cancelled or postponed. The storm center finally moved out of the plains into Illinois with a vengeance. Illinois Central train No. 372 was traveling south from Clinton, IA on Jan. 21, when the IC trainmaster, Vergil Shelley, of LaSalle realized the dire situation that was developing.

The drifting snow had become so bad that some cars on Rt. 52 south of Sublette were buried in drifts nearly eight feet high. Only the tops of some vehicles were still visible. Drivers were stranded in Lee and Bureau counties. Shelley walked three miles to Sublette to intercept the oncoming train. Once there, he instructed Walter Olson, the engineer, to add a caboose and a couple of freight cars to house the stranded motorists.

Local farmers were also out trying to find drivers lost in the snowstorm. Those they found were taken to the train or to the Sublette community hall to wait out the storm. Others who made it to the train were taken back to the stations in Amboy and Dixon. In Sublette, firemen, church groups, and Boy Scouts took on the job of feeding the stranded travelers. Mr. L. M. Dinges, owner of the grocery store, provided the food. Sublette families provided shelter to married couples.

Snowplows finally cleared Rt. 52 the next day, but most Illinois highways were still snow-packed and slippery. Those who found shelter in Sublette were able to return to their vehicles. The 5.7-inch snowfall was the first big storm of the year.

PITY THE BUSINESSMAN AND BANKER

The generosity of small town folks, like those in Sublette, was not shared by others, who would rather take from others instead of helping them. Only two weeks before the January snowstorm, an individual sat down with Elmer Maier, the vice president of the Seneca Community State Bank, to discuss some property. Suddenly, the man pulled out a .45 and instructed Maier to fill a sack with the bills in the cashiers' drawers. Then he locked Maier and the bank bookkeeper, William Steep, in a back room. Fleeing quickly in his brown Chevy, the robber seemed to make a clean getaway with $964.

However, the robber's conscience was bothering him so much he simply turned himself into the police the next day. The man was a prominent community leader and member of the Morris school board, Maynard Davis. He readily confessed to the crime explaining that he was in debt. "I lived beyond my means; I spent more than I earned. I had $6,000 in debts, a little more than my yearly income."

Other thefts were not as easy to solve. On March 1, the Mendota Kroger store was robbed. A month later on April 4, two men stole $2,000 from the Leo Classon supermarket. It was just about closing time when a man walked into the store with a sawed-off shotgun and demanded the cash from the registers of Gerry Bader, 16, and Gary Bentley, 18. A third clerk Jim Bryan, 16, was told not to make a move. The gunman also went into the office to take money from the safe. The gunman then joined his accomplice at the store entrance and calmly walked to their car. In spite of roadblocks set up by Mendota, Peru, and LaSalle police, the robbers escaped.

Four months later in August, the same individual robbed the Classon store again. During the holdup, the robber was distracted by Ivan Smith, a customer who was coming into the store with his son. While the bandit was distracted, Mr. Classon, the owner, managed to shove a second sack containing $800 into a customer's shopping bag. The gunman took the remaining sack containing only $300, and he grabbed Smith and his son. He forced Smith to drive him to the Mendota Hospital parking lot. There, the bandit freed Smith and his son; got in his own car parked in the lot; and made his getaway. Mrs. Edgar Ehlers, discovered she had taken home the sack containing the $800 and returned it to Classon.

The A&P supermarket in Marseilles suffered a more substantial loss. Around midnight on Feb. 6, a fire was discovered at the grocery store. Several individuals renting apartments above the store, located next to the Mars Theater, had to be evacuated. They lost all of their clothes and furnishings. The fire was very intense, and water pressure was dropping. Fire Chief John Armstrong ordered his men to lay out a hose running 1,500 feet to a backwater area of the Illinois River for additional water. The firemen labored from midnight until noon the following day to control the blaze. Although there was a firewall between the A&P and the theater, smoke and water damaged the theater. The estimated damage amounted to more than $100,000. The Peerless cleaners, located next to the theater, also suffered smoke damage.

DISASTER PREPAREDNESS

While fires always presented significant disruptions in the social life of small towns, local communities continued to prepare for even worse calamities. In Princeton, civil defense classes had been conducted for several weeks. Upon completion of the 14 lessons conducted over the course of a month, participants were well versed in the subject of Cobalt 60, one of the radioactive hazards faced from nuclear fallout.

In the LaSalle-Peru-Oglesby area, Civil Defense Director Curtis Clay announced the appointment of an assistant, Alex Ptak of Peru. An organizational meeting for those interested in joining an auxiliary police force at the Peru VFW hall was scheduled for early February.

Another program, the Radio Amateur Communications Emergency Service (RACES) was organized under the direction of Edward Remmith and his assistants, Gordon Currie and William Adrian. The combination of a Tri-Cities, Streator, and Ottawa RACES program would provide radio communications during state and national exercises.

Another program of the civil defense training involved radiological training at L-P High School. Physics teacher Orville Bauer and Floyd Hybki, who trained in the Army in radiological warfare classes, were the instructors.

In March, Spring Valley reactivated its civil defense unit. Mayor William Savitch, the unit coordinator, and Dr. Henry Jacobs, the program director, spoke to 20 deputy directors on Mar. 24. Dom Marchiando, a deputy director with experience in radiation detection, explained the use of Geiger counters. Twelve individuals had already completed the radiological classes held at the city hall.

Two members of the local Civil Air Patrol, Carl Blum and Rube Burington, were appointed air-watch deputy directors. Each of the deputy directors reviewed his responsibilities ranging from police and fire safety to housing, transportation, and welfare.

THE RING AROUND CHICAGO

Local civil defense was an important part of preparedness, but few would have ever thought that Wenona's old coal dump would be the site of a radar installation making up part of the Chicago Air Defense System. For years, the country depended on the Ground Observation Corps to watch for low-flying Russian bombers because of the lack of a sufficient number of radar units. During July 1957, Capt. E.J. Arnold and Sgt. L. Cobb of the 45th AAA Brigade in Chicago came to Wenona to evaluate the dump as a possible location for a radar unit that would plot any planes in the area around Chicago. On Jan. 14, the following year, Maj. A.G. Prondzinski was making final arrangements to lease a 4-5 acre site. Wenona was a perfect location for one of the Army's radar installations spread across Illinois, Indiana, Wisconsin, and Michigan. The radar units would encircle the Chicago-Gary-Milwaukee industrial area with an early warning network.

In late February, the Keno Construction Co. of Highland Park began to cut down the top 30 feet of the 125-foot dump to create a flat area for the radar antenna and two support buildings. The latter would be used to house radar equipment, office space, a day room, and an emergency generator. The excess dirt was pushed over the side of the dump to use as fill for the road.

By early March, a spiral road was constructed from the bottom to the top of the slag pile so the soldiers could ride in jeeps to the facility on top. A road was also graded around the base of the dump, and a barbed-wire fence was erected around the hill to prevent unauthorized access. On Mar. 13, a USAF helicopter carrying four officers on an inspection mission landed in the Wenona school parking lot. A crowd gathered since this was the first time a helicopter had landed in the town.

Facilities for the soldiers were on the second floor of the Goodwin Brothers building, which was remodeled to provide sleeping quarters, a dining room, kitchen, and office. Some of the soldiers had apartments in the Hotel Stanton. The old coal mine office became the supply and maintenance shop.

Twelve soldiers were on site by April 10, 1958 when two generals, Maj. Gen. Eugene Cardwell, Fifth Region commander, and Brig. Gen. Peter Schmick of the 45th AAA Brigade flew to Wenona by helicopter to inspect the facility.

The Army held an open house for the public on April 18. Two Army station wagons were used to take civilians to the top of the hill. While the radar looked rather small from the base of the hill, many of the visitors were surprised to see how large the antenna really was. Thousands toured the barracks and radar facility that day.

A 20-man military detachment, consisting of men from the 45th AAA Brigade and the 105th Signal Corps, was assigned to maintain and operate the facility. Once the unit became operational, the radar scanned the skies within 200 miles of Wenona. Because of the heavy air traffic around Midway Airport in Chicago, the Wenona post commander, M/Sgt Carroll Dow, assigned two men to watch the radar screens. Any unidentifiable planes were reported to the Nike base at Arlington Heights.

The radar antenna on the summit of the coalmine slag pile measured 15-feet high and 40-feet wide. It revolved 360^0 six times a minute.
Wenona Index photo.

One of the men assigned to operate the equipment was Spc/4 Russell Martin (at right). He had trained as a radar operator while stationed in Japan and received orders to report to the Wenona site. When he arrived, the facility was ready to operate. According to Martin, as many as five men at a time were at the radar site.

The Wenona radar site did not operate 24 hours a day but instead had various hours of operation. According to Martin, most of their work occurred during the evening hours. Most of the time, the men watched conventional air traffic flying into Chicago's Midway Airport, but occasionally, they would engage in an Air Defense Exercise (ADX). This was a simulation activity used to test the men on their response time in identifying and reporting unidentified aircraft. At Wenona, they had a direct phone line to Arlington Heights, the Army post that directed the operations of a ring of Nike anti-aircraft missiles around Chicago.

There were occasions when a slow moving plane was detected and did not respond to the Identification – Friend or Foe (IFF) challenge. Although the target was usually a farmer flying over his fields or other small plane, the soldiers in the Wenona radar building could not take a chance. It was difficult to determine the type of plane. The blip on the screen could easily be a low flying enemy bomber. The unit would notify the anti-aircraft center in Arlington Heights, and a flight of F-100's were scrambled and flown to the target area for a positive identification. Sometimes the jets flew directly over Wenona, according to Martin.

When Wenona radar identified aircraft not responding to IFF signals, F-100 Super Saber interceptors like this one were ordered to investigate.
USAF photo.

CWO Elmer Decker was in charge of the Illinois radar units at Wenona, Dixon, and Rossville, south of Hoopeston, and Logansport, IN. Other radar sites were located in Michigan and Wisconsin.

The Dixon site was located at the old WWII Green River Ordnance Plant (GROP) northwest of Amboy. On Jan.

27, the Dixon Telegraph learned of the Army's plans from Lt. Col. Alex Pharitonoss, information officer at 5th Army Command in Ft. Sheridan. He said the Army would send a 10-20 man detachment to operate the radar unit. A temporary unit had been operating at the GROP site in 1957. The more permanent facility was expected to be complete by the spring of 1958. The Corps of Engineers had sent representatives to Dixon to find a building to house the men. Actual construction of the installation was scheduled for mid-February with a completion date of April 1.

Capt. Henry Sellers of the 61st AAA in Milwaukee came to Dixon in February to complete the final details. He estimated the small detachment could add $6,000-$7,000 a month to the local economy. The facility would include a radar pad, a ready-crew building, and a generator building. The Dixon site was one of the ten sites, which extended in a circular pattern from Tisch Mills, WI around to Luddington, MI.

The Dixon radar unit was ready for its first inspection in early April. Maj. Gen. Eugene F. Cardwell and Brig. Gen. Peter Schmick flew to the facility by helicopter. Sfc. Fletcher Owens, head of the 12-man radar team, took the officers on a tour of the facility and the house at 607 N. Galena, where the men were housed. Like the Wenona radar site, information from Dixon was sent to Arlington Heights, which could alert the area's Nike batteries.

Three of the 21 Nike missile batteries in the Chicago area were located at Orland Park. Some of the other launchers in the southwest Chicago suburbs were located at Homewood-Flossmoor, Lemont, and Worth-Palos. Each battery had four missile launchers. These sites were capable of tracking targets within a 100-mile range and provided about a half-hour warning time of approaching hostile aircraft. The missiles themselves were located in underground bunkers about a mile from the command center and were only partially armed. It only took the missile technicians a matter of minutes to arm the weapons and bring them to their vertical launch positions. The base commander had to give the final order to launch a missile.

This Nike-Hercules missile on display at Golden State NRA, CA was typical of the missiles surrounding the Chicago-Gary area. Additional batteries were positioned around Milwaukee and other major cities. National Park Service photo.

To prevent the accidental interception of friendly aircraft, there were positive identification controls, but the exact nature of the method of identification was classified. The men at each missile site had to have security clearances, and the technicians were sent to Redstone, NM to practice actual firings at unmanned aircraft.

During the first year, some of the soldiers at the Wenona site had been discharged or reassigned, and new men took their places. CWO Clyde DeClue, the commanding officer of the 105th Signal Corps detachment, and several other men had brought their wives and families to live in Wenona. Many of the soldiers had taken an active role in community activities. For the Independence Day celebration in 1959, Lt. Dinsel flew to Wenona in a helicopter. The Army also displayed a Nike missile. The chopper pilot was photographed with the celebration queen, Miss Rita Luckey, near the missile.

The Army's radar installation in Wenona did not last very long. In September 1959, officers from the 45th AAA Brigade decided it was time to remove the radar installation. The slag pile was collapsing causing cracks in the foundations of the generator building and the operations building. According to the chief radar operator, Sgt. Wilson Roach, the heavy equipment used in the initial construction to level the top had cracked the weathered crust, and erosion was causing the hill to shift. They planned to find another site for the radar equipment and anticipated removing the antenna and associated equipment sometime in October.

The removal of this defense installation did not seem to bother towns surrounding Wenona even though they were not totally prepared to respond to a Soviet attack. The Illinois Civil Defense Command sent a letter to 23 local towns pointing out their failure to install air raid sirens. The towns listed in the letter included Cedar Point, Dana, Earlville, Grand Ridge, Kangley, LaSalle, Leland, Leonore, Lostant, Oglesby, Ottawa, Marseilles, Mendota, Peru, Rutland, Seneca, Sheridan, Streator, Tonica, Triumph, Troy Grove, Utica, and Wedron. The LaSalle County Board of Supervisors simply decided to file the letter and depend on local residents to tune their radios to the CONELRAD radio frequencies for instructions in case of a national alert. Apparently, only those citizens listening to the radio or watching TV would know there was an alert.

THE GREAT FLOOD OF 1958

Mother Nature also posed a threat to cities and villages in the Illinois Valley. It seemed that about every eleven years, a major flood engulfed several towns and the bottomlands along the Illinois River. On July 13, record-breaking rainfall measuring 5.49 inches in the Illinois Valley was to blame for the rapid rise in the Illinois River and nearby creeks. The deluge beat the Oct. 11, 1931 record by over an inch. The river level at Shippingsport Bridge rose eight feet overnight. On Sunday, it measured 13.75 feet. Rising almost a foot an hour, by early Monday morning, it had risen to 21.72 feet.

Hardest hit were the towns of Ottawa, Utica, and Peru. For Ottawa it was the worst flooding since 1917. L-O-F Glass workers returning after their plant's closure during vacations were not able to get to the plant due to flooded streets. It was also impossible to drive through the business district of Utica. The creek in Utica overflowed its banks at 3 a.m. Boats were used to evacuate isolated homeowners. Canteens were set up in Utica and Peru to provide food to homeowners, who were forced to evacuate. On Mill Street in Utica, the water depth varied from six to twelve inches. Telephone and electrical services were knocked out, but Illinois Bell sent a crew from Morris to restore service. Illinois Power customers waited several hours before electricity was restored. Because of possible water contamination, Mayor John Kidd issued a boil order.

Elaine and Colleen Weiden waded through the swirling waters in front of Bauman's grocery store and the Utica post office.
Utica library collection.

A News-Tribune photographer captured this photo of men wading through the business district of Utica with a canoe. Those who could be identified were Jerry Dettore, Don Ketter, Bob Barndhart, Ronnie Davis, Bernard Payne, Bill Goetch, Randy Holdcraft, and Dan Carey.

The heavy rains also affected Peru and LaSalle. In Peru's Centennial Park, a deep ditch at the southwest corner was filled with water to a depth of 30 feet. The L-P High

School stadium was flooded with three feet of water. There was some concern as the rains continued that the west wall might collapse. Assessing the damage the next day, a News-Tribune reporter described the field as better suited for water polo than football. The concrete base for some of the stadium seats was washed out causing the wooden seats to splinter. The raging waters could not flow fast enough through a culvert and created a huge hole under the north wall.

Construction on the new Peru bridge was also affected. Although piers four and five had been poured, some of the steel was under the floodwaters. Once the 265-foot steel span was assembled, it would be floated on a barge to the bridge site.

Marquette Cement superintendent Ralph Moyle sent home 150 workers. He was afraid the rising waters of the Vermilion River would threaten the pump. During the night, two of the cement barges had broken loose from their moorings.

City workers in Oglesby worked to pump out the water filling the basement of the Illinois Power substation on South Columbia Ave. The switching equipment there was vital to providing electricity to Oglesby, LaSalle, and the surrounding area. Working through the early morning hours, the workers made some progress in reducing the water level.

The heavy rainfall had a serious effect on the entire region to some extent. Rt. 6 east of St. Margaret's Hospital was partially blocked by gravel washing into the street. The Deer Park golf course was described as a "swimming pool."

Residents living in Wenona basement apartments were forced to vacate. The west end of town looked like a lake, and the motors on oil burning furnaces and other appliances were damaged. Farmers in the area lost some of their livestock.

The situation was even worse for residents in Streator and Sparland. Some lives were lost, and there was extensive property damage according to the Wenona Index.

In Putnam County, an earthen dam constructed to create a fishing lake above the farmland owned by Joseph

Englehaupt gave way. The waters of the lake behind the dam washed away the hillside but spared the Englehaupt house.

At Starved Rock State Park, the park custodian wakened 15-20 campers at 4 a.m. They only had an hour to get out before the rising waters covered the campground. The river crested on July 15 at about 10 a.m. The Starved Rock lock tender reported the river was still 17 feet above normal. Down river at the Shippingsport Bridge, where the depth is typically 12 feet, William Boehm, the bridgetender, said the river depth was 24.8 feet. Flood stage was 26 feet. River traffic was tied up at both locations. Barges loaded with grain and scrap steel were in danger of sinking. A coal barge, owned by Marquette Cement sank after breaking free from its moorings on Monday night.

Barges were jammed against the gates at Starved Rock dam during the 1958 flood. The ferry *Illini* capsized and was pinned against gate number four at the Starved Rock dam. Oglesby library collection.

The flood was also thought to have indirectly caused a major explosion in Streator on July 14. Police speculated that the rising waters of the Vermilion River possibly caused sewer gas to back up into in the four-story Williams hardware store, and a spark from some source ignited the gas. There were at least 16 people in the store at the time of the explosion, which blew out the front of the store and sent the roof over the elevator shaft flying. A number of bodies were found in the rubble. Among the dead were Don Williams, the store owner; Allen Williams, the owner's 16 year old son; Miss Selma Hultman, a bookkeeper at the store; Ray Aschinger and George Blaine, two clerks at the store; and Vernon Rush. Other bodies were seen under a pile of fallen bricks on the second floor, but it was too dangerous to try to remove them because of the weakened condition of the structure.

GONE IN A FLASH

Of the various crimes committed in the Illinois Valley, the one that "woke up half the town" of Ottawa was the mysterious explosion that destroyed the popular 671 Club located at Rt. 6 and Rt. 71. On July 21, just before midnight, Peter Morello reported a fire at the nightclub. Morello and Jerry Monroe and their dates, Mary Ann Brockman and Karen Hardin, were driving by the club when they saw the flames and stopped at a nearby house to use the phone. At 11:45 p.m., there was a tremendous explosion knocking the Marseilles boys to the ground. Falling debris from the explosion crushed the top of their car with the girls inside. They were taken to Ryburn Hospital. Others in the area were injured in the blast. Fire departments from Ottawa, Marseilles, and Naplate came to extinguish the fire, but there was little left of the structure.

After a four-month investigation, Walter Parlier, the deputy state fire marshal, could only conclude that some unknown individual(s) had set the fire. His conclusions were based on several facts. There was a smell of kerosene, and ammonium nitrate was found beneath the sill of the southeast door. All the pilot lights on the gas stoves were inspected and operating correctly. In addition, a witness had seen a car backed up to the southeast door of the club only minutes before the explosion. "The evidence discloses this fire was created by burning kerosene," Parlier said.

THE LINCOLN-DOUGLAS CENTENNIAL DEBATE

Ottawa was known for its appreciation of its role in the history of the United States. Perhaps the most notable event to involve Ottawa was the 1858 debate between Senator Stephen Douglas and Abe Lincoln. One hundred years later, the city fathers and other leaders turned the centennial of that famous event into several days of celebration.

The festivities began on Thursday, Aug. 21. Local children participated in three events, a costume parade, a pet parade, and a bicycle parade. Later in the afternoon, a crowd estimated at 2,500, gathered in Washington Park to watch a re-enactment of the historic debate between Lincoln and Douglas. The crowd gathered near the site of the original debate. On the speakers' platform, Edward F. Claus reiterated the remarks by Douglas, and Quentin Pletsch repeated the words of Lincoln.

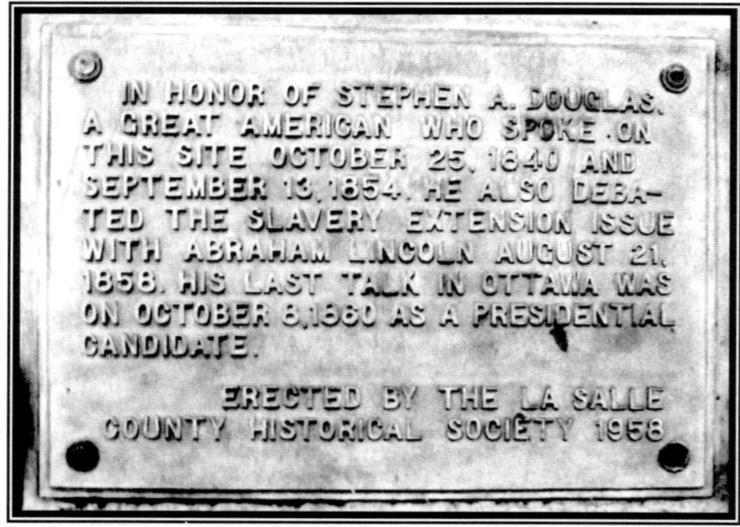

As part of the Ottawa observance, representatives of the LaSalle County Historical Society unveiled this bronze plaque dedicated to Stephen Douglas. It is displayed at the north entrance of the county courthouse. Photo by author.

That evening, 3,200 hungry participants were eager to enjoy the dinner being served by the Ottawa Jaycees. In addition to cooking 1,700 pounds of ribs for the barbeque, the Jaycees served 700 pounds of vegetables, 90 gallons of applesauce, and 90 gallons of coffee according to the Ottawa Times. The dinner was a real bargain for only $1.00.

Ads reprinted from the Ottawa Republican Times.

On Friday, Aug. 22, one of the major events was a historical pageant, "Abraham Lincoln – Through All the Years." The play, depicting 14 major events in the life of Lincoln, was performed at the Armory. Among those participating were the members of the Valley Circle Theater, the Rock Island Railroad chorus, the Ottawa American Legion chorus, the Ottawa H.S. choir, the Ottawa Women's Club Chorus, and choral groups from Wedron and Sheridan.

Activities on Sunday included the opening of an antique car show on Lincoln Place in front of the city offices at noon. The children had the opportunity to see a free showing of "Young Mr. Lincoln" at the Roxy.

The adult parade started at 2 p.m. and lasted almost two hours. Streator's float carrying "Lincoln" and "Douglas" won first prize. Ottawa's city float, featuring the Liberty Bell, came in second in the judging. An All-Star baseball game began after the parade. The evening events included a competition between eight drum and bugle corps entries on King Field and a second showing of the play.

HOW LONG WILL IT LAST?

One story reported in the local newspapers for over half a decade was a road construction project paralleling Rt. 6. Engineers decided the weather in north central Illinois was so varied it would make an excellent location to determine the long-term effects on various types of paving materials and construction techniques used in building highways. The American Association of State Highway Officials (AASHO) project began with preliminary studies and continued with the actual construction of several test loops of roads using different materials, such as concrete and asphalt.

There was much work to complete before the first trucks began the actual driving in 1958. In April 1955, survey work began for the test road, which would be located from a point a half mile north of the Rt. 6 and Rt. 178 junction and extending for nine miles to the east. Within that area, the project called for the construction of four two-mile loops. Two other smaller loops were also constructed. It took about a year to purchase a 300-foot right-of-way to enclose the wide turns at the end of each loop.

In August 1956, the earthmovers began grading. Two steel bridges and two concrete bridges were constructed across the test loops. These were built on Terra Cotta Road, Naplate Road, Osage Road, and Lone Tree Road.

The winter weather of 1957 halted construction, but in the spring of 1958, plans were made to hire hundreds of workers to complete the project by that summer. A substantial number of the new hires were engineers and junior engineers from Illinois and surrounding states as well as civil engineering students from several universities.

Banked curves were created at the ends of the loops to facilitate turns by the heavy rigs. Photos by Bob Little.

One side of each large loop was paved with concrete; the other side had asphalt pavement (see diagram on pg. 217).

The base under the concrete or asphalt was constructed with a variety of materials layered in different thicknesses. Photos by Bob Little.

As the construction work neared completion in April 1958, Col. Albert A. Wilson of the 48th Transportation Group was given the road test assignment. The 400 soldiers of the 10th Medium Truck Co. were transferred to Illinois with 70 trucks.

This aerial view looking east shows four of the six loops and gives some idea of the size of the project. The AASHO buildings are located at the bottom of this picture. Photo supplied by Gene Smania.

The soldiers were billeted at a facility called Wallace Barracks, located west of Rt. 23 and north of Ottawa. The living area included a barracks, mess hall, day room, dispensary, and PX. In addition, the facility provided a crafts department, darkroom, barbershop, and TV room.

The Wallace Barrack's facility included a mess hall at left, which connected to the buildings where the soldiers lived. Photo by author.

According to Bob Thrush, owner of the property where Wallace Barracks was located, this house was occupied by the commander of the 48th Transportation Group during the AASHO testing program. Photo by author.

After a month of training with empty trucks to "condition" the new pavement, drivers started carrying loads of concrete blocks weighing 2,000 to 48,000 pounds. The loads depended on whether the trucks were single or tandem axle vehicles.

Trucks ranged in size from ¼-ton to 5-ton diesels to determine the durability of different highway construction designs. Photo by Bob Little.

AASHO truck photo by Bob Little.

The trucks operated over four 6,000-foot loops with six vehicles in each lane. Soldiers were scheduled to drive six days a week in three shifts, one driving; one resting; and one with time off. They would drive 50 minutes each hour in two nine-hour periods each day regardless of the weather.

To avoid the boredom, each soldier was trained to operate each of the various types of trucks; drive on each of the loops; stop for a ten-minute rest break every hour at the control point on the loop, and take a half-hour lunch break.

This is one of the trucks used to carry the heavier loads. Notice the solid concrete blocks holding the smaller blocks in place. Photo by Bob Little.

215

The test road was officially opened on Wednesday, Oct. 15, 1958. At the ribbon cutting ceremony, Ellis L. Armstrong, commissioner of the Bureau of Public Roads, U.S. Dept. of Commerce, described the project as "The most important road in America today." At the conclusion of the speeches to a crowd of 200 guests, a flare was fired, and the Army trucks starting rolling on the loops.

Within minutes of the noon inauguration, the project had its first injury. One of the drivers slipped and hit his head when he jumped from the cab of his truck to the ground. He was treated at the Wallace Barracks' dispensary and taken to Ryburn Hospital for observation. The trucks did not began rolling again until 4 p.m.

Another problem developed just as the evening crew was about to begin its work. Traffic on Loop E was halted "indefinitely." A section of the loop had already crumbled where asphalt was laid down over dirt. It was not surprising because there was no sub-base preparation. In addition, two of the bridges over the loops began to sag.

After only an hour of evening driving, a tractor-trailer overturned as the driver crossed the steeply banked curve at the end of a loop and tried to stop at one of the service areas. The driver was uninjured, but the vehicle was demolished. The load of 48,000 pounds of concrete blocks was scattered around the test area. That was enough for the Army officials. All operations were cancelled until a complete investigation was made of the mishaps. The day was soon known as "Black Wednesday."

A number of the concrete blocks once carried by the test trucks are still found at the IDOT truck garage along I-80. Photo by author.

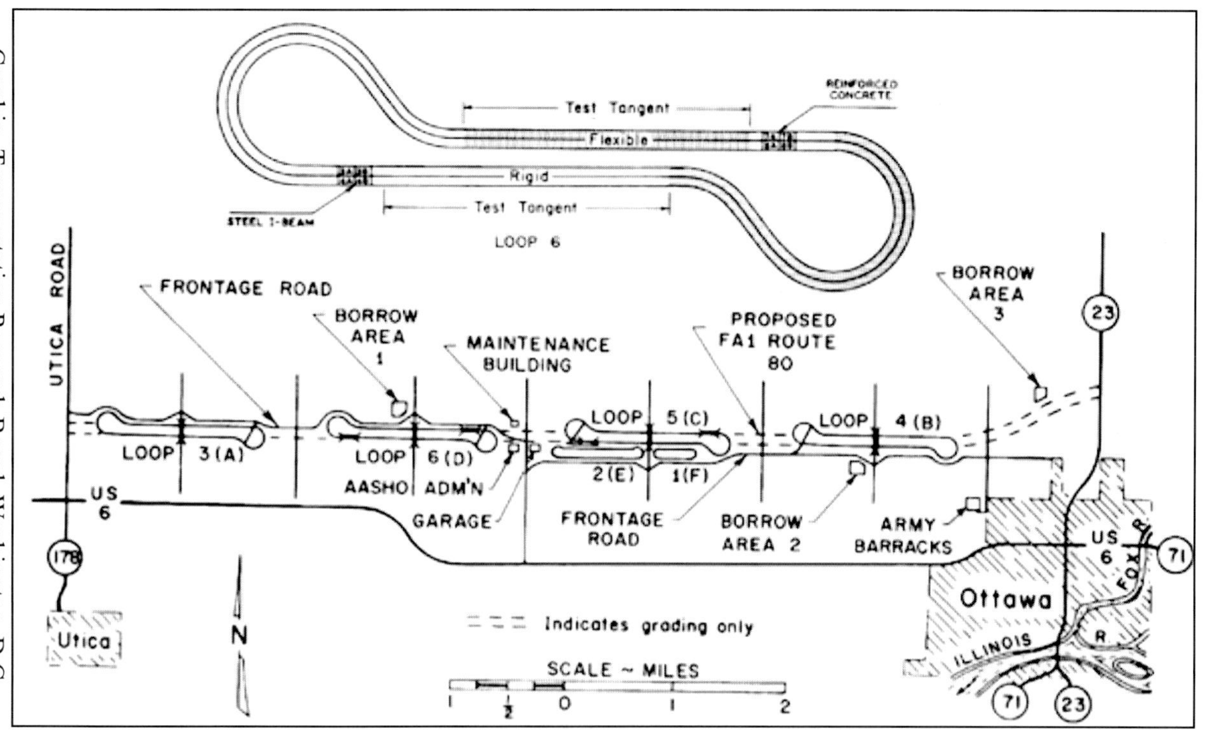

Graphic - Transportation Research Board, Washington, D.C.

The resumption of driving did not begin until early November. One change instituted because of the tractor-trailer wreck was the redistribution of the concrete blocks to lower the center of gravity. Furthermore, each driver was required to complete supervised training to familiarize them with the characteristics of the vehicles they were going to drive.

While on the daily drives on each loop, drivers watched for "traffic signals," which indicated the number of times they had circled a loop in one lane. After completing a certain number of miles, the signals would change and the drivers would use the other lane.

Soldiers drove their trucks on the newly completed test loops with little to distract them from the monotonous views of miles of cornfields.

By the end of the year, many local people had been hired for the project. About 100 employees came from the Ottawa-LaSalle area. Henry C. Huckins of 1205 Jefferson St. Ottawa was named supervisor of the instrument lab. Another Ottawan, William R. Milligan, of 500 West Main became the assistant operations manager.

The soldiers and civilians working on the test road did not remain outsiders but, in many cases, were actively involved in community organizations. Some bought houses and those with families sent their children to the Ottawa Catholic and public schools. The soldiers also formed their own bowling league made up of six teams. Although those in charge of the project promised an "open house" for the community, the weather interfered and that event was tentatively planned for the spring of 1959. However, the event did not take place until the fall.

THE DAY THE RUSSIANS CAME TO TOWN

Cold War apprehensions were calmed somewhat when a delegation of Russian scientists and engineers came to Ottawa on Nov. 24, to observe the operations at Union Carbide's Bakelite plant. Union Carbide Vice President C. W. Blount had visited the USSR in June and served as the group's American tour guide. Since the Russians spoke little English, translators accompanied the group. Signs were printed in Russian to label the equipment at the Bakelite plant. They had numerous questions about the plant equipment and asked for drawings of the equipment. Midwestern businesses and farms continued to draw Russian visitors. The following summer, a delegation headed by the First Deputy Soviet Premier Frol Kozlov visited the James Holderman farm near Morris.

A BITTER END TO 1958

On the evening of Dec. 3, a fire of undetermined origin destroyed the Methodist church built in 1906 in Paw Paw. The one-story building was leveled; the loss was estimated at $150,000. Only the entrance and chimney remained. Republican Times photo.

In early December, an Arctic blast swept through the Illinois Valley bringing with it snow and single digit temperatures. Starved Rock officially reported a temperature of 16^0 below zero at the locks. At Marseilles, it was 14^0 below while rural areas reported lows of 20^0 below zero. LaSalle County was covered with five inches of snow.

In spite of the frigid conditions, the tows on the Illinois River were still moving. The Starved Rock Lockmaster, H. W. Hart, said it would take at least two more weeks of the sub-zero temperatures before tows would be affected. Ice on the river was over five inches thick. The maintenance crew kept the ice chipped off the lock's gates. However, it was taking about twice as long, a half hour, to move tows through the locks.

WINTER'S ICY GRIP CONTINUED

The winter weather continued to be miserable in January. The next winter blast came on Jan. 20. Six inches of snow was accompanied by 30-mph winds, rain, and sleet. A number of church dinners and other events were cancelled.

The next morning, LaSalle buses were stuck in snow banks on the north side of the city. Cars were stuck in drifts in both LaSalle and Peru. Fortunately, Peru had its snowplows out early in the storm so the city streets were relatively clear. According to Mayor Bruno, LaSalle only had one snowplow capable of handling the heavy snow. Homeowners had to dig through four-foot drifts to get to the streets. Rt. 6 in Bureau County was down to one lane. Putnam County roads were slippery and dangerous, and all rural schools were closed.

It was a similar situation in LaSalle County, where 21 rural schools remained closed. These included the schools in Wedron, Sheridan, Wallace, Fall River, Serena, Dayton, Deer Park, Craft, Milton Pope, Ophir, Earlville, Waltham, Lostant, Leland, Rutland, Freedom, Mazon, Kangley, and Mendota. The public and most parochial schools in the cities remained open. More snow was predicted for the following night.

The strong winds whipped the 7.5-inch two-day snowfall into deep drifts virtually paralyzing the Tri-County area. According to the Westclox weather station records, the snowfall was second only to the 13.1 inches that fell Feb. 7-8, 1933. The Feb. 24-25 storm in 1950 was almost as bad as the current snowfall but fell short of the record by .1 of an inch. The total on the ground in early January was 9.5 inches.

Road conditions had hardly improved. In Sandy Ford and Leonore, the blacktops were covered with drifts six to eight feet deep. Gravel roads throughout the Tri-Counties were virtually impassable. Rt. 51 was clear as far north as Rt. 30. Motorists found if they could get that far, the rest of the highway to Chicago was clear. However, driving south was another matter. Rt. 29 was closed between Henry and Peoria.

Snowplows on Shooting Park Road found six cars buried together in a drift. Their owners had simply abandoned their vehicles. Other intersections jammed with cars included the intersection of Rt. 23 and Rt. 52, where 20-30 cars were abandoned. Another group of cars was found under the snow at Meriden. To compound Peru's problems, two of their snowplows broke down and had to be taken in for repairs. How could it get any worse? On Thursday night, the temperature dropped to 9^0 below zero!

In spite of the Arctic-like conditions, the snowplows got the job done, although it was necessary to call in a Caterpillar bulldozer from Trompeter Construction Co. to remove the snow in Peru. Even it lost a track during the snow removal effort.

James Schmidt, the information officer at the AASHO site, said they had to stop driving the Army vehicles for two days during the worst of the storm. Although the diesel engines were hard to start, they were soon back to the normal routine

One man singled out for his outstanding service during the blizzard was Ernest Stuart of 954 Sixth St. in LaSalle. The mail clerk at the LaSalle post office used his ham radio to maintain service on the Illinois Central RR when the telegraph lines between the Clinton terminal and the LaSalle depot were

out of service. He relayed train orders for 14 consecutive hours during the worst of the storm. Stuart was assisted by John Vasicak, an Oglesby teacher and radio "ham," who handled radio communications during the nightshift.

News-Tribune photo of Ernest Stuart at his radio published on Jan. 23, 1959.

In spite of the terrible weather, Buzz Verucchi booked some of the best talent available. Buddy Holly was scheduled to perform on Feb. 7, 1959, for the club's Winter Dance Party, but he was killed in a plane crash along with Ritchie Valens and J.P. Richardson, "The Big Bopper," They had decided to fly ahead of the rest of their troupe. Their small plane crashed in a farm field 15 miles northwest of Mason City.

Rather than disappoint hundreds of patrons, Verucchi was able to book a relatively new singer, Frankie Avalon. While teenagers would never hear Buddy Holly's live rendition of "Peggy Sue" or "It's So Easy to Fall in Love," the show still went on Feb. 7 featuring Frankie Avalon with his first big single, "Venus."

Tommy Sands was another young star who performed at the Les Buzz Ballroom. Photos and show bills contributed by Dick Verucchi.

THE BATTLE OF BREWERY HILL

Throughout the decade, there were frequent labor problems. In January 1959, a jurisdictional strike shut down the Star Union Brewery and the Star Bottling Co. in Peru. The labor action pitted the Teamsters against the United Construction Workers, UMW Local 846. The company was caught in a power struggle. The Star Union management really didn't care who represented the workers in the plant.

An unidentified striker walks the picket line at the Star Union Brewery. News-Tribune photo published Jan. 16, 1959.

The brewery workers reported for work but honored the UMW picket line. The Teamsters were determined to have their local represent all the workers and refused to allow trucks to load any of the plant's production.

At times, the confrontations between the two unions became heated during the strike, which began on Jan. 9. On Jan. 15, forty Teamsters from Springfield, Decatur, and other locations came in an eight-car caravan and drove through the brewery worker's picket lines. While Local 846 hurriedly sent for reinforcements, the Peru police arrived. The confrontation between the two union groups was tense, but after standing in the frigid air for a couple of hours, the Teamsters decided to back off and left.

In spite of their apparent setback, the Teamsters were encouraged by an announcement that both of the Star Union plants recognized the Teamsters as the sole bargaining agent for the truckers. This meant the plant workers would have to cross any UMW picket line and return to work on Jan 19. The management asked the Teamsters to have six drivers at the brewery and two deliverymen at the soft drink plant. James Hoffa of the Teamsters asked the court to force the officers of the brewery local to turn over the books and any union funds of the brewery union to him.

Everything looked fine on paper until Monday morning when the workers refused to cross the picket line. A temporary settlement was worked out so that a small group of men could cross the line to complete the "brew" begun on Sunday and prevent spoilage. Teamsters were also allowed to begin deliveries. Furthermore, an announcement by the company that the management was taking applications for new workers seemed to indicate the pickets would be ignored since they were no longer company men.

All workers were told to return to work on Wednesday at 1 p.m. However, when the hour arrived, there was another confrontation by the pickets of Local 846, who turned the workers away.

Standing in front of their makeshift shelter, Star Union Brewery pickets kept warm with hot coffee boiling on their coal-burning stove. News-Tribune photo Jan. 21, 1959.

The strike dragged on into February; neither side was willing to compromise. A citizens committee headed by Mayor Robert Potthoff tried to mediate. However, it was not long before the mayor quit that position saying that the group had outlived its usefulness. On Feb. 14, eight production workers crossed the six-man picket line at 6:45 a.m. This surprising move seemed to threaten the effectiveness of the pickets who called for reinforcements. An hour later, ten more men joined them on the line. The Teamsters responded by sending a caravan of cars from southern Illinois carrying 34 men. The cars converged on the plant from two different directions. The pickets tried to stop the cars by pulling a log and a metal half-barrel across the driveway. Neither obstacle did much good as the cars pushed them out of the way and filed into the parking lot. When the police and the mayor finally arrived on the scene, one picketer complained he had been struck by a car. Others said the men, who went into the brewery, were armed. A police search of the vehicles and the men on the picket line did indeed reveal a few weapons. Mayor Potthoff, who was described as "a combat general" by the News-Tribune, called for additional police. They were quickly on the scene with tear gas bombs and a four-inch fire hose, which the police connected to a hydrant. "We got 90 pounds of pressure, and if trouble starts, somebody is going to be drowned," declared the mayor.

The loading dock of the old Star Union Brewery on Pike Street was the site of the confrontation between the brewery workers and Teamsters in 1959. Photo by author.

Both sides, the Teamsters inside and the UMW picketers outside the plant, exchanged insults for the next two hours. The confrontation came to a head when a Ziebert truck backed up to the loading dock and was surrounded by picketers. Violence was averted after John Clinch, the company lawyer, spoke to the driver, and he drove away up Pike street hill. Clinch told the men gathered at Pike and Brewster streets, "This is the end of the battle of brewery hill. At any rate, the fighting from here on out is going to be done in a courtroom. I'm going to make no more attempts to put the brewery back in operation." The Teamsters then returned to their cars and drove away too.

The battle moved into the courts in March with the Brewery Workers Union petitioning the National Labor Relations Board (NLRB) to hold a certification election that could result in a decision making their Local 33 the sole bargaining agent. On Mar. 19, their representative, Harold Davis, demanded both plants resume production immediately. Otherwise, it would be considered a lockout in which case he insisted the men be paid.

From that point on, the violence subsided. The NLRB intervened and began holding interviews that lasted for months trying to determine if a certification election was warranted. In any case, the famous Battle of Brewery Hill was over. The News-Tribune compared the seriousness of the confrontation to the murders associated with the 1916 cement strike and the closing of the Apollo metal works due to mob action during the Depression.

Access to Star Union beer certainly wasn't a problem for 54 young people who got caught in a police raid on May 1, in the basement of the Dom Lounge at 1059 First St. in LaSalle. The police found four half-barrels of Star Model beer. Admission tickets for the "all the beer you can drink" party were sold to the boys for $1.50 and $1.00 for the girls. In addition, there was gambling

in the form of "Jar-O-Do" tickets found in the possession of Tom Whalen, 17, of Spring Valley. Two other smaller beer parties were raided that same weekend. One group of teens was found at St. Vincent's Cemetery, and another group was arrested at the LaSalle Drive-In.

Buzz Verucchi offered an alternative to the underage drinking problem. After booking Duane Eddy and Dale Hawkins on the Friday night of the big beer bust, Verucchi was able to schedule the newest teen idol, 16-year old Fabian, for the Saturday, May 9 show.

This News-Tribune ad said parents should accompany their teenagers to the performance. Verucchi promised there would be no drinking of any kind at the show.

The day after the show, about 150 young female fans besieged Fabian's automobile as it pulled up to the curb at the News-Tribune office. The screaming girls pressed so tightly against the car door that extra police had to be summoned to help Fabian get into the building. In an interview with a reporter, Fabian explained how he had a rather hectic lifestyle. He had a show in Lincoln, NE on Friday night, and on Sunday night, he had to be in Columbus, OH for another performance before heading back to his high school classes in Philadelphia. His summer was already booked for his role in the 20th Century Fox movie, "Hound Dog Man." While being interviewed, some of his female fans climbed on the building's windowsills trying to catch a glimpse of teen star. Although there was no time for autographs during his departure, the admiring girls mobbed him again in spite of the rain.

NO TIME FOR A BEER PARTY

While teenagers found time to party, adults had more serious concerns. On Friday, April 17, the sixth annual Operation Alert was in full swing to test nationwide civil defense preparedness. The units throughout Illinois had a 2½-hour warning of the impending attack and then faced the consequences of a simulated nuclear bombing of eight major cities in the state. Springfield had the distinction of being bombed twice.

Once the warning was received, all FM and TV stations went off the air for a half hour. Nationwide, over 2,600 AM stations also ceased broadcasting at 10:30 a.m. Locally, WLPO stayed on the air since it was designated as a CONELRAD station. However, instead of the usual broadcast on 1220 kcs., the program was broadcast on 1240 kcs. Normal programming resumed at 11 a.m. Students at L-P High School participated by evacuating the school. Part of the simulation involved finding locations to house the estimated 170,000 casualties evacuated from cities hit by atomic bombs.

As Operation Alert continued on Saturday, civil defense inspectors stopped all cars at a roadblock north of Peru to practice checking for imaginary radioactive contamination. An attack on Rock Island would have resulted in radioactive fallout being dispersed over the Illinois Valley. A decontamination crew wearing protective suits and carrying Geiger counters at the Midway Plaza Shopping Center inspected vehicles and passengers for radioactivity.

Homeowners were expected to remain home and have sufficient food and water to last for two weeks. In addition, a first aid kit and battery-powered radio were recommended for each household. As a precaution, homeowners were told to turn off their water and gas valves. One member of each family was supposed to have had instruction in first aid to take care of minor injuries. More serious injuries would be handled in a 200-bed field hospital supplied from Seneca. Trucking companies were also assigned to move casualties to medical facilities.

Princeton's Perry Memorial Hospital and the Princeton schools were actively involved in the test. All patients at the hospital were informed of the alert through the intercom. The hospital switched over all electrical power needs to a recently installed generator. Doctors and department heads were all placed on a standby alert during the practice. The children in the Princeton elementary school grades 4-8 were given copies of the alert scenario so they would know what to do. At Princeton H.S., science teacher Walter Bright had instructed his senior students in the use of Geiger counters and dosimeters. Periodically, announcements were made to all the students about the progress of the scenario. The Red Cross used the high school gym to care for simulated casualties.

OPEN HOUSE AT THE AASHO ROAD SITE

While civilians had their periodic civil defense training, the soldiers at the ASSHO project continued their routine circling around the test loops. Their work was largely ignored by the public until May. A five-hour open house was held on Armed Forces Day, May 16, so the public could have a close-up view of the various types of trucks that continued to circle the loops. During the tours conducted by Army personnel, civilians could visit the Data Processing Center and the Materials Testing Lab, where concrete beams and cylinders were tested every 15 minutes. The test loop immediately west of the Administration Building was shut down so that buses could take civilians on the same loops as the soldiers had been driving on for months.

Wallace Barracks was also open for visitors to display

the Army's support activities for the road project. There were also displays by the National Guard, the Army Reserve Recruiting Branch, Red Cross, American Legion and VFW. A complete Army field kitchen was also set up. Visitors could refresh themselves with cold drinks.

By September, the soldiers had completed four million miles on the test loops. Put into the context of the new space age, that was the equivalent of 17 trips to the moon.

This IDOT aerial survey of the old AASHO shop building and truck garage was taken May 12, 1987. Photo provided by Gene Smania.

The buildings used by AASHO personnel are still used by IDOT today. Although some additions and renovations have been made, they are essentially the same as they were during the 1950's and 1960's testing program. Photo by author.

Drivers of thousands of semis, cars, and other types of vehicles drive on I-80 each day with hardly a glance at the AASHO weather loop between Ottawa and Utica. Although no longer needed, this remaining loop has become a historical monument to the engineering research used to build the nation's interstate system.

The weather loop as it appeared in January 2010. Photo by author.

Engineers wanted to see not only the effects of weathering on different types of material but also how different lengths of the concrete pours were affected. No traffic operated on the weather loop. In this 2010 photo, asphalt in the foreground covers one section while the rest of the roadway was concrete poured in specific lengths. Photo by author.

Pictured are the crumbling remains of the AASHO weather loop (1F), so-called because it was left in place to evaluate the long-term effects of weathering on highway pavement. The broken pavement in the foreground on the last remaining loop shows the effects of weathering and subsequent vegetative growth on the aging concrete poured in the 1950's. Photo by author.

Engineers could also determine the results of weathering by cutting out sections of eroded concrete. The holes were filled with asphalt. Photo by author.

FIRES SWEEP THROUGH LOCAL COMMUNITIES

While the long-term destruction of roads was being examined in the AASHO project, a series of devastating fires destroyed many buildings in communities in LaSalle and Putnam counties during the summer of '59. The village of McNabb lost a quarter of its business district in an early morning fire on June 6. Rudy Happold, a McNabb fireman, discovered the blaze at 4:30 a.m. It apparently began in the basement of the McNabb Food Center and quickly spread to Grasser's Hardware Store. Fire Departments from Magnolia, Tonica, Lostant, and Granville responded to assist the men in McNabb. It was a dangerous fire for the men since they also faced exploding rounds of shotgun shells and rifle bullets. In the grocery store, cans of food were exploding and flying high into the air sometimes dropping down on spectators in the street. A steel fire door prevented the flames from destroying the variety store owned by Mario Sabino.

Collapsing walls crushed the L.W. Swain recreation parlor in McNabb. News-Tribune photo.

Another major fire took place a month later in Ottawa. On July 6, at 2 a.m., a blaze swept through the 800 block of the business district destroying five stores, Mayme Reardon's women's apparel, Kline's Department Store, Ferley's Jewelry Store, Feltman's Gift and Toy Store, and the Piggly Wiggly grocery store. The fire was thought to have started in the middle of the block at Feltman's and spread to buildings on either side. Firemen evacuated 30 residents occupying 15 apartments above the stores. While hundreds of Ottawan's watched, the front of Kline's and Feltman's collapsed into LaSalle St. around 6 a.m. By 9 a.m., only the front wall of the grocery store remained standing. Other businesses damaged due to smoke and water included the Fashion Shoe Store, Todor's Variety Store, Montgomery Wards, the Elks Club, and the Colwell apartments. The fire was described as the most destructive commercial fire in Ottawa since 1881.

A fire destroyed the same area on Dec. 9, 1930 when the Gayety Theater and a number of other businesses burned. The theater was later replaced by the Roxy Theater.

In this News-Tribune photo of the Ottawa fire, the southwest corner of the Piggly Wiggly store crashed into the street.

A third major fire occurred in August. Starting in the Illinois Laundry and Cleaners at 719 Columbus, the flames spread to the roof of Norem's Buick garage. Although Ottawa firemen quickly controlled those flames, smoke began to rise from the roof of the 70-year old First Baptist Church at Jefferson and Columbus. Soon, the entire roof was engulfed. Firefighters using twelve leads of hoses fought for eight hours to bring the fire under control.

Only the brick and stone walls of the church, which was built in 1890, were still standing. The interior was gutted. A new church was built at a different site. News-Tribune photo Aug. 27, 1959.

MAGNOLIA GOES DRY

While many buildings suffered water damage due to fires, the 250 residents of Magnolia faced a fire threat from the lack of water. The village well had gone dry in August, and the 70 families in the village had to resort to old shallow wells for their drinking water. But, these too were going dry. As soon as it was apparent that something had gone wrong with the village well, which had been drawing water from a depth of 223 feet, the Wright and Hagemen Drilling Company from Henry was hired to bore a deeper hole. After days of drilling finding only layers of shale, they reluctantly pulled the bit out at 245 feet. Some residents speculated that a new well might have to be drilled to the west of the village.

Finally, one last effort was attempted. On Aug. 15, the drillers were able to bring in a flow of water. It was temporarily unusable for drinking until the State Department of Health certified it was safe for consumption, but the threat of fire without a water supply was greatly alleviated.

GOOD TIMES RETURN

The benefits of future nuclear power plants to produce inexpensive electricity focused on research conducted during the summer of '59. Illinois Power Co. hired Sargent and Lundy Engineering, to construct a simulated nuclear reactor at the utility's Hennepin property. They built a containment shell measuring 14 feet in diameter and 32 feet long. The vessel was placed vertically in the ground near the coal-fired power plant with only the very top exposed. A smaller steel drum, measuring 3.5 feet in diameter and 23 feet long, was inserted inside the shell. Illinois Power engineers prepared to determine the results of a possible rupture of the inner vessel containing pressurized boiling water. If the inner vessel failed, a cold water supply was available to mix with the steaming water within seconds. The science of nuclear reactors was still in the experimental stage, and the tests conducted in Putnam County were important in the development of nuclear power plants.

On Aug. 17-18, Mendota held its 12th annual Sweet Corn Festival, an occasion never to be forgotten by Miss Sue

Munson, the 17-year old queen, who was crowned by Marjorie Angler, the 1958 queen. Fifty tons of corn were served at the Kroger store parking lot following the annual parade.

Another young person who would always remember the summer of '59 was Gary Lee Moreland, 13, of rural Princeton. The Illinois Valley youngster represented the region in the All-American Soap Box Derby.

In a 2010 interview, Gary said his father, Bill Moreland, was one of his main supporters, who offered advice in constructing a soapbox racer. Gary, who was sponsored by the News-Tribune, the Valley Jaycees, and Balestri's Garage, won the Spring Valley Derby to qualify for the national competition in Akron, OH.

Gary Moreland arrived in Akron, on Aug. 15 for the 22nd soapbox derby sponsored by Chevrolet. Officials in Akron named a street after him during the week-long activities. Photo provided by Gary Moreland.

Vice President Nixon was among the thousands of spectators to see Gary Moreland in Lane 2 win his first heat in Akron. By the end of the day,

Gary had finished 57th among the 170 boys in the races. Gary said he could have done even better, but he forgot his oil can. He said his car design and lubrication with 90W oil were the secrets of his success in the races. Photo by Bill Moreland.

STRIKES IMPACT LOCAL INDUSTRY

The Peru brewery strike during January was just one of many labor disputes during 1959. In August, the International Chemical Workers Local 79 at Carus Chemical was in its tenth week of a strike that started on June 6. Less controversial than the brewery confrontation, the men wanted an hourly raise and better benefits. A peaceful resolution was agreed to, and the men went back to work on August 24. The new contract provided a 9¢ hourly raise and improved fringe benefits. Those jobs requiring specialized skills, such as machinists and employees in the hydroquinone process received more.

The nationwide steel strike, which had been going on since July 15, affected many Illinois Valley firms. That month, Local 5212 of the United Steel Workers rejected an offer from New Jersey Zinc in DePue. Their contract had expired on June 21, but without a resolution, the union announced a strike on July 27. They asked for a 10¢ hourly raise, but the company was only willing to offer an increase of 8¢ per hour. The DePue workers had not seen a raise since 1956.

By October 1959, the steel strike was increasing concerns of local manufacturing plants. Illinois Valley companies that required steel in their manufacturing included the Anthony Manufacturing Co., TIMCO, and the Knoedler Manufacturing Co. in Streator, and American Nickeloid in Peru. In Ottawa, the H. K. Porter Co. and LaClede-Christy plants were barely coping with the prolonged work stoppage. Also affected more directly were the sand companies in Ottawa, including Ottawa Silica Co. and Bellrose Sand Co., which provided molding sand for steel castings. Orders had been cut by as much as 40 percent. Fortunately, the L-O-F plant had stockpiled glass anticipating a resurgence of orders for the automobile industry as soon as the strike ended. Management at the Peltier Glass Co., a supplier for Ford Motor Co., reported a need to cut production due to a decline in orders. Still, there had been no major layoffs. However, one of the local companies finally feeling the effects of the strike was the Marathon Electric Manufacturing Corp. at Earlville. Of the 370 employees, over 300 men were laid off.

The 116-day strike lasted until Jan. 15, 1960. In the meantime, the American steel industry lost market share to imported steel products from Japan and Korea.

REMEMBERING THE MINERS

Programs of remembrance of the terrible 1909 fire at the Cherry coal mine were conducted every year. The 50th anniversary in 1959 was well attended. On Sunday, Nov. 15, memorial services were held at Holy Trinity Church and at the Congregational Church. The Spring Valley Municipal Band, American Legionnaires from LaSalle, Spring Valley, Princeton, Buda, and Cherry, the Cherry Fire Department, Boy Scouts, UMW members, and dignitaries participated in the afternoon march to the cemetery. John Ghizzoni, who represented the UMW, said, "Many of our present mine safety rules and much compensation legislation are a direct result of this terrible disaster in the Cherry mine." A wreath was laid at the miners' monument by Mrs. Marguerite Hynds Abrahams of Decatur, daughter of William Hynds, who died in the disaster, and Kathleen Baldini and Margie Reinsch, whose grandfathers were killed in the 1909 fire.

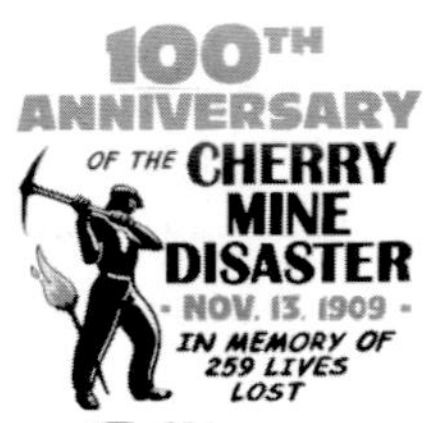

Some of the individuals who participated in the 50th anniversary of the tragedy filled the streets of Cherry on the 100th anniversary to recall the sacrifice of the 259 men and boys, who died in the 1909 fire. Photo by author.

LOOKING BACK AT THE DECADE

The decade of the 50's cannot be summed up in a single theme as could the 1920's with prohibition; the 1930's with the crippling unemployment of the depression; or the 1940's fighting in WWII. Yes, there were still military concerns. The fighting in Korea put hundreds of local men in harm's way once again. The Cold War with the Russians fostered a fear of nuclear war as residents read weekly reports of the detonation of nuclear bombs in the Nevada desert. Military installations in Wenona, Dixon, and rural Streator reminded residents that war was a real possibility. A call for civilian volunteers to watch for enemy bombers and annual civil defense exercises heightened tensions. The outbreak of hundreds of flying saucer reports early in the decade only compounded popular fears especially since neither the military nor the government adequately explained the occurrences to those who witnessed the phenomena.

Besides those concerns, social changes affected children and adults. The polio epidemic, whose victims were largely children, gradually waned with the development of the Salk vaccine. Gambling began to disappear as slot machines and pinball machines were confiscated from local taverns. The big casinos in LaSalle were closed, but residents still found enjoyment in annual summer festivals, big name bands, and rock and roll vocalists. Troubling stories of local bank robberies, murder, historic floods, winter blizzards, and devastating fires filled the newspapers. Labor disputes with local industries and railroads became part of the ebb and flow of the local economy.

Transportation innovation was also noteworthy especially with the development of the Rock Island RR's *Jet Rocket*. At the end of the decade, the AASHO test loops became a showplace, attracting scientists and highway engineers from around the world to examine the long-term effects of vehicles on highway construction.

All of these stories described the decade of the 50's as a unique period in the history of the Illinois Valley.

Ron Bluemer is a Cold War veteran. He served with the USAF Security Service and Strategic Air Command. After receiving a teaching degree at Illinois State University, the Chicago native moved to the Illinois Valley with his wife, Peggy, in 1967.

The author has lived in Granville for the last 43 years. During that time, he became a distinguished educator having taught history and science in the Putnam County schools from 1967 to 2001. Following his retirement, Bluemer continued his passion for teaching as an instructor at Illinois Valley Community College, where he teaches courses in U.S. History and Western Civilization. In addition to his literary work, Bluemer is also a freelance reporter for the LaSalle News-Tribune and a well-known public speaker.

His books on the Illinois Valley include **Black Diamond Mines** (2001), which documents coalmine operations from Braidwood to Spring Valley. **Rails Across the Heartland** (2002) describes the major railroads in the Illinois Valley. **Speakeasy** (2003) focuses on the prohibition era of the 1920's and ties to organized crime. **Casino** (2004) exposes the illegal gambling centered at LaSalle, IL. **Home Front: WWII in the Illinois Valley** (2005) describes the wartime involvement of citizen soldiers. **Here Comes the Boat!** (2005) provides nostalgic views of canal boats on the I-M and Hennepin canals and the steamboat trade on the Illinois River. **Rails Across the Heartland** (2006) is an expanded version of the 2002 edition. **Fire Below**! (2007) provides a factual account of the Cherry mine disaster of 1909. **Buddy, Can You Spare a Dime**? (2008) is a very timely book published at the beginning of the Great Recession of 2008-10. It describes the 1930's Great Depression and the jobs created by FDR. **Back to the 50's** (2010), the author's latest book on the Illinois Valley, covers a variety of topics from the Korean War to the advent of rock and roll entertainment.

Several of the newer books are still available through Grand Village Press at 134 Cleveland Circle in Granville, IL.